THE VEDANTA-SARA

THE VEDANTA-SARA:

WITH

AN INTRODUCTION,
NOTES,

AND

AN EXAMINATION OF ITS CONTENTS.

TRANSLATED

BY

DR. J. R. BALLANTYNE

GYAN

Published by

Gyan Publishing House
5, Ansari Road
Daryaganj, New Delhi-110002
Phone: 011-47034999, 9811692060
E-mail: books@gyanbooks.com

Distribution Network
gyanbooks.com
India, USA, Canada, UK, Australia

ISBN: 978-93-6208-235-0 (HB)
First Published, 1898

2nd Impression 2024

Printed at: Gyan Press, Delhi.

THE VEDANTA-SARA
Translator: J. R. BALLANTYNE

THE

VEDANTA-SARA:

TRANSLATED

BY

DR. J. R. BALLANTYNE,
Principal,
SANSKRIT COLLEGE, BENARES,

WITH

AN INTRODUCTION,

NOTES,

AND

AN EXAMINATION OF ITS CONTENTS.

"The Vedanta, the highest conclusion of Indian thought, is based on a mistaken and pessimistic view of life; on a formulated dogma unsupported by any evidence and untaught in the hymns of the Rig-Veda: the whole an elaborate and subtle process of false reasoning."—Rev. T. E. Slater, *Studies in the Upanishads*, p. 47.

FIRST EDITION, 3,000 COPIES.

THE CHRISTIAN LITERATURE SOCIETY FOR INDIA:
LONDON AND MADRAS.

1898.

NOTE.

The References to the Upanishads are taken from *Hindu Pantheism,* by Colonel G. A. Jacob, who has also kindly read the proofs of the following pages. In addition to the *Concordance to the Upanishads,* the following works have been prepared by Colonel Jacob:

a. Hindu Pantheism (Trübner's Oriental Series.)

b. *Mahānārāyaṇa-Upanishad,* with Commentary (Bombay Sanskrit Series.)

c. Sureśvara's *Naishkarmyasiddhi,* with Commentary (Bombay Sanskrit Series.)

d. Eleven Ātharvana-Upanishads, with Commentaries (Bombay Sanskrit Series.)

e. *Vedāntasāra,* with 2 Commentaries. (Nirṇayasāgar Press.)

CONTENTS.

THE VEDANTA-SARA.

INTRODUCTION.

Carlyle says: "Of a man or of a nation we inquire first of all: What religion they had? Answering this question is giving us the soul of the history of the man or of the nation. The thoughts they had were the parents of the actions they did; their feelings were the parents of their thoughts: it was the unseen and spiritual in them that determined the outward and the actual; their religion, as I say, was the great fact about them."

Man is a religious being: *he will worship*. In whatever part of the world he may be found, however degraded in many respects, he has a religion of some kind or another.

India is now the scene of a momentous revolution. Railways, education, the press, and contact with the West are producing vast changes. Of all, the most important are those connected with religion. It is true that comparatively few are yet thus affected; the masses are largely untouched. But the new ideas will filter down, and gradually influence the whole. Lyall thus indicates the probable course of events:

> "It seems possible that the old gods of Hinduism will die in these new elements of intellectual light and air as quickly as a net full of fish lifted up out of the water; that the alteration in the religious needs of such an intellectual people as the Hindus, which will have been caused by a change in their circumstances, will make it impossible for them to find in their new world a place for their ancient deities. Their primitive forms will fade and disappear silently, as witchcraft vanished from Europe, and as all such delusions become gradually extinguished." [1]

An effort is now being made to prevent the "old gods of Hinduism" from dying in the "new elements of intellectual light and air." This has been tried even in the case of Krishna. All such attempts will be as fruitless as those made to arrest the decline of polytheism in Europe.

Educated Hindus generally profess to be adherents only of the "Higher Hinduism." By this is understood the VEDANTA or the eclectic system of the BHAGAVAD GITA.

It is very desirable that the followers of every religion should have an accurate acquaintance with its principles; and know the

[1] *Asiatic Studies*, pp. 299,300.

light in which it is regarded by intelligent men of the present day. The Vedánta is at least two thousand years old. Much knowledge has been accumulated during that long period. Students of the Vedánta should not only know what Veda-Vyasa actually taught, but what is thought of his system viewed in the light of the nineteenth century. To aid them, a summary is given in the following pages of the *Vedánta-Sútras* and a complete translation of the *Vedánta-Sára*, the next standard on the subject. Explanatory notes, from the best Orientalists, are added where necessary, and there is a complete examination of the system. The whole has been revised by Colonel G. A. Jacob, author of *Hindu Pantheism*, and *a Concordance to the Upanishads*, one of the first European authorities on Hindu Philosophy.

THE BHAGAVAD GITA may be regarded as the loftiest production of Hindu religious thought. It contains some noble sentiments, beautifully expressed; but it teaches polytheism and pantheism, besides claiming a divine origin for caste. An English translation of the complete work is given in the publication noted below.[1]

To enable the reader to form his own judgment of Vedántism, one of the standard treatises is given in full, followed by an examination of its doctrines.

ORIGIN OF HINDU PHILOSOPHY.

Intellectual Growth.—"The life of a nation," says Morell, "bears an obvious analogy to that of the individual."

The child gives life to every object around it. Whatever strikes the imagination affords delight; the most extravagant tales are accepted as true.

"The severing of imagination on the one hand from abstract principles on the other, marks the rise of another era in a nation's development,—that, namely, which corresponds with the sphere of THOUGHT, properly so called. The separation is effected by the understanding, and is marked by a decided tendency to metaphysical speculations.

"When these periods have run their rounds, then the age of positive science commences,—that in which the reason gathers up all the results of the other faculties, and employs them for the direct investigation of truth."[2]

---

[1] THE BHAGAVAD GITA, 8vo. 108 pp. 4 As. Post-free, 5 As. An English Translation, carefully revised; numerous Explanatory Notes, and an Examination of its Doctrines. Sold by Mr. A. T. Scott, Tract Depôt, Madras.

[2] Morell's *Elements of Psychology*, pp. 263, 264.

The Hindus, in general, represent the childhood of humanity. Every thing around them is instinct with life. "The idlest legend," says Professor Cowell, "passes current as readily as the most authentic fact, nay, more readily, because it is more likely to charm the imagination; and in this phase of mind, imagination and feeling supply the only proof which is needed to win the belief of the audience."

The tendency to metaphysical thought, the speculative stage of the human intellect, may be called the "childhood of philosophy." In Hinduism, this may be described as the religion of the Upanishads, the Darśanas, and Bhagavad Gítá.

There is no sharp line of demarcation between popular and philosophic Hinduism. They blend into each other. Some combine the two. Even the common people are leavened, more or less, with some of the notions of philosophic Hinduism.

The "Age of Positive Science" is yet represented in India by only a handful; but the minority will grow.

Course of Hindu Thought.—India was first occupied by non-Aryan races, generally like the wild tribes still found in various parts of the country, although some had attained an elementary civilisation. Their religion apparently consisted in propitiating the demons and tutelary gods; and this, to the present day, forms the actual cult of the masses.

The Aryans poured in from Central Asia through the western passes, and spread over the great river-basins of the Indus and Ganges, where they gradually became mingled with the pre-existing population, the two races mutually acting upon each other.

In later Vedic times the Indian tribes were gathered together in farms, in huts of sun-dried mud, in houses of stone, in hamlets, and in fenced towns, under village chiefs and Rajas. The outward aspects of their life were not unlike those of rural India of to-day. The Indians of the Vedic age tilled their rice and barley, irrigated their fields with water courses, watched the increase of their flocks and herds, and made a hard or easy livelihood as blacksmiths, wheelwrights, boat-builders, weavers, doctors, soldiers, poets, priests. They lived upon the produce of their cattle and their fields, drank wine and soma juice, and exercised their leisure in sacrificial feasts, in games, and spectacles.

The powers of nature present themselves to them as so many personal objects. The child personifies the stone that hurts him; the child of superstition personifies the laws of nature as gods. Sky and Earth are the father and mother of gods and men. Mitra, presiding over the day, wakes men, and bids them bestir themselves betimes, and stands watching all things with unwinking eye. Varuna, ruling the night, prepares a cool place of rest for all that move, fashions a pathway for the sun, knows every wink of men's eyes, cherishes truth, seizes the evil-doer with his noose, and is prayed to have mercy on the sinful. Agni, the fire-god, bears the oblation aloft to the gods. Indra, ruling the firmament, overthrows Vritra; Soma invigorates the gods, and cheers mankind.

The gods require to be flattered with hymns, to be fed with butter, to be refreshed with soma juice, that they may send rain, food, cattle, children, and length of days to their worshippers. Life is as yet no burden; there is nothing of the blank despair that came in later with the tenet of transmigration, and the misery of every form of sentient life. Pleasures are looked for in this world; their harvests are enough for the wants of all; their flocks and herds are many; and pleasures are looked for again in the after-life in the body in the kingdom of Yama.

So far from life being regarded as a curse, "May you live a hundred winters!" was looked upon as a benediction.

This worship of the personified powers of nature with a view to material benefits gradually hardened into a series of rites to be performed by the priesthood. In course of time it came to be held that the sacrifices performed without knowledge of their import produced their desired effect,—some material good, the birth of children, long life, or future happiness. This later form of Vedic religion received the name of the *Karmakáṇḍa*, or ritual department of the Vedas.

But in the midst of this life of the primitive Hindu, there are discernible the first stirrings of reflection. Questions began to be raised in the hymns of the Rishis in regard to the origin of earth and sky. One of them asks, "Which of them was first and which was later? You wise, which of you knows?" Another asks, "What was the fruit, what the tree, out of which they cut the sky and earth?" In one hymn earth and sky are the work of Viśvakarman. In another it is Hiranyagarbha, the golden Germ, that arose in the beginning; in another it is Varuna. Agni is sometimes the son of Earth and Sky; at other times he is said to have stretched out the earth and sky. In a few of the later hymns there are touching confessions of ignorance; such as, "Who truly knows or who has told what path leads to the gods?"

"This creation, whether any made it, or any made it not? He that is the overseer in the highest heaven, he indeed knows, or haply he knows not."

The period of the hymns was followed by that of the ritual and legendary compilations known as the Bráhmanas. Of these Bráhmanas, particular portions, to be repeated only by the hermits of the forests, were styled Aranyakas, and to the Aranyakas were attached the treatises setting forth as a hidden wisdom the fictitious nature of the religion of rites, and the sole reality of the all-pervading and all-animating self, or Brahman. This hidden wisdom, the philosophy of the Upanishads, in contradistinction from the *Karmakáṇḍa*, or ritual portion, received the name of *Jnánakáṇḍa*, or knowledge portion of the Śruti, or everlasting revelation. There were now virtually two religions, the *Karmamárga*, or path of rites, for the people of the villages, living as if life with its pleasures were real, and the *Jnánamárga*, or path of knowledge, for the sages that had quitted the world, and sought the quiet of the jungle, renouncing the false ends and empty fictions of common life, and intent upon reunion with the sole reality, the Self that is one in all things living.[1]

Rise of Hindu Pessimism.—Dr. Murray Mitchell says:

"With them (the Upanishads) commences that great wail of sorrow which, for countless ages, has in India been rising up to heaven. All the earlier Vedic hymns take a cheerful view of life; but with the Upanishads we see the beginning of that despondency which, as time goes on, will deepen almost into despair."[2]

Three causes may be assigned for this:

1. After the Aryans had settled in India for some time, they began to feel the influence of the hot, enervating climate. Labour was a burden, undisturbed repose seemed the highest bliss.

2. "The unhappiness of the environment. Warfare was almost the normal state of Indian society;—war with the aborigines; war of one Aryan tribe with another; a long struggle between princes and priests, and steady exaltation of the latter; the rise and rapid progress of Buddhism; war with Scythian hordes;—in all this there was undoubtedly enough to distract and depress the Indian mind."[2]

3. Chiefly, the belief in transmigration. Of this there are only the faintest traces, if any, in the Vedas. It is uncertain whether the idea sprang up in the Hindu mind, or was derived from the aborigines, Dr. Murray Mitchell inclines to the former supposition.

The pessimistic feeling was intensified by Buddha. The first of the "four noble truths" which he professed to have discovered is that "Existence is Suffering." As a devout Buddhist counts his beads, he mutters *Anitya, Dukha, Anatta,* "Transience, Sorrow, Unreality."

Prince Mahanama thus describes to his brother Anuradha the alternate happiness and misery of life:

"The being who is still subject to birth may at one time sport in the beautiful garden of a dewa-loka, and at another be cut to a thousand pieces in hell; at one time he may be Mahá Brahmá, and at another a degraded outcaste; at one time he may eat the food of the devas, and at another he may have molten lead poured down his throat; at one time he may sip nectar, and at another he may be made to drink blood. Alternately, he may repose on a couch with the dewas, and writhe on a bed of red-hot iron; enjoy the society of the dewas, and be dragged through a thicket of thorns; bathe in a celestial river, and be plunged in

---

[1] Abridged from Gough's *Philosophy of the Upanishads*, pp. 7-17.

[2] *Hinduism, Past and Present*, p. 48.

the briny ocean of hell; become wild with pleasure, and then mad with pain; reside in a mansion of gold, and be exposed on a burning mountain; sit on the throne of the dewas, and be impaled with hungry dogs around; drawn in a chariot of the dewas, and dragged in a chariot of fire; he may now be a king who can receive countless gems by the mere clapping of his hands, and now a mendicant, taking a skull from door to door to seek alms."

Monier Williams says:

"Transmigration is the great bugbear, the terrible nightmare and daymare of Indian philosophers and metaphysicians. All their efforts are directed to getting rid of this oppressive scare. The question is not, What is truth? Nor is it the soul's desire to be released from the burden of sin. The one engrossing problem is, How is a man to break this iron chain of repeated existences? How is he to shake off all personality?"

All systems of Hindu Philosophy are pessimistic. The *Brahmavádin* says:

"Every system of Hindu philosophy starts with the conviction that individual existence is a journey full of torments from death to death, that the individual soul is tossed about, as result of its errors, ignorances, and sins, from life to life, from billow to billow in the great ocean of transmigration, that desire is the motive power that makes for the eternal continuance of life, that this desire has its root in ignorance or the non-discrimination of the true nature and value of things, that the law which fetters living beings to the existence in the world *can* be broken and that salvation from *samsára*, or the cycle of life and death, can be attained by spiritual knowledge of the eternal verities. These great ideas form the woof and the warp of Indian thought, permeating its whole outlook, its attitude towards life, its most sacred aspirations and its most cherished wishes and hopes." May 22, 1897.

The popular feeling is the same. In every Indian bazar the expression may be heard almost daily, "This is the Kali Yuga," the Iron Age. The venerable Vedic Rishi, Parásara, in the Vishnu Purána, thus describes some of its evils:

"The observance of caste, order, and institutes will not prevail in the Kali Age . . . Men of all degrees will conceit themselves to be equal with Brahmans, cows will be held in esteem only as they supply milk. The people will be almost always in dread of dearth, and apprehension of scarcity, they will all live, like anchorets, upon leaves, and roots, and fruits, and put a period to their lives through fear of famine and want. . . Princes, instead of protecting, will plunder their subjects . . . women will bear children at the age of 5, 6, or 7 years; and men beget them when they are 8, 9, or 10. A man will be grey when he is 12; and no one will exceed 20 years of life."[1]

What a sad contrast to the Krita (Golden) Age, when the fruits of the earth were obtained by the mere wish, and men lived four thousand years!

[1] Wilson's Translation of the *Vishnu Purána*, pp. 622, 624.

THE SIX SCHOOLS OF HINDU PHILOSOPHY.

"The Upanishads contain the first attempts to comprehend the mysteries of existence; and their teachings cannot be gathered up into an harmonious system. But as time went on, a desire was felt to expand, classify, and arrange these earlier utterances—to make them more definite and more consistent. Hence gradually arose what we may call the official philosophy of India, which is comprised in a number of methodical treatises. These are generally called the six *Darśanas*, or 'exhibitions.[1] No doubt it was only by degrees that they assumed their present elaborated shape, which cannot be much older than the Christian era."[2] They consist of the following:

1. The *Nyáya*, founded by Gautama.
2. The *Vaiśeshika*, by Kanáda.
3. The *Sánkhya*, by Kapila.
4. The *Yoga*, by Patanjali.
5. The *Mímánsá*, by Jaimini.
6. The *Vedánta*, by Badaráyana or Vyása.

The original text-books of the various systems consist of *Sútras*, which are held to be the basis of all subsequent teaching. The word properly signifies 'a string.' We may understand it to denote a string of rules, or rather aphorisms. "They are expressed with extreme conciseness—doubtless for the purpose of being committed to memory; and without a commentary they are exceedingly obscure."

The Darśanas belong to the division of Hindu books, called *Smriti* (that which is remembered). They are therefore authoritative; but not to the same extent as the Vedas and Upanishads, which are termed *Sruti* (heard).

"It is usual to classify these systems in pairs, making three pairs in the order given above; but this arrangement is not satisfactory. The Nyáya and Vaiśeshika may indeed go well enough together; and the Sánkhya and Yoga may with some difficulty do the same; but the Mímánsá and Vedánta have very little in common. Their conjunction has arisen from the circumstance that the Mímánsá (otherwise called the Púrva or Earlier Mímánsá) deals with the ritual portion of the Vedas as explained in the Bráhmanas; while the Vedánta or Uttara (later) Mímánsá seeks to unfold and apply the principles of the Upanishads; and thus, as each expounds a portion of what had come to be called the Veda, the two systems came to be bracketed together."

"None of the six systems professedly attack, or deny, the authority of the Vedas: on the contrary, they all profess the profoundest reverence for the sacred books. It is difficult to see how the authors of some of the systems could do this with sincerity. Yet the Hindu mind has long

---

[1] Or "Demonstrations of Truth." Sir Monier Williams.

[2] *Hinduism Past and Present*, p. 53.

surpassed all other minds in the ability to hold, or believe itself to hold, at the same time, two or more opinions which appear to be wholly irreconcilable: indeed an acknowledged note of the Hindu mind is 'eclecticism issuing in confusion;' it has been said to be 'the very method of Hindu thought.' But the contradictions among the philosophical systems were too glaring to escape the notice of men capable of reflection; and accordingly the author of one Darsana and his followers frequently attack the supporters of the others. Thus the great controversialist Sankara denounces a follower of the Nyáya philosophy as a bullock *minus* the horns and tail—implying, we suppose, that he had all a bullock's stupidity without his power of fighting. The author of the Sánkhya charges the followers of the Vedánta with 'babbling like children or madmen.' The Mímánsá accuses the Vedánta of being disguised Buddhism. The Padma Purána maintains that four of the six systems are simply atheism.

"But while thus radically opposed to each other, the six official systems of philosophy are all held to be orthodox."[1]

1. The Nyaya.

Gautama, the founder of this system, is claimed to have been a Rishi, married to Ahalyá, the daughter of Brahmá. She was seduced by Indra, who had to suffer in a way too indecent to be mentioned.

The word Nyáya signifies "going into a subject," taking it, as it were, to pieces. The system was intended to furnish a correct method of philosophical inquiry into *all the objects and subjects* of human knowledge, including, *amongst others*, the process of reasoning and laws of thought.

The different processes by which the mind arrives at true and accurate knowledge are four; viz.—*a.* *Pratyaksha*, 'perception by the senses;' *b.* *Anumána*, 'inference;' *c.* *Upamána*, 'comparison;' *d.* *Śabda*, 'verbal authority,' or 'trustworthy testimony,' including Vedic revelation.

'Inference' is divided into five *Avayavas*, or 'members.' 1. The *pratijná*, or proposition. 2. The *hétu*, or reason. 3. The *udáharana*, or example. 4. The *upanaya*, or application of the reason. 5. The *nigamana*, or conclusion. The following is an example: 1. The hill is fiery; 2. for it smokes; 3. whatever smokes is fiery, as a kitchen-hearth; 4. this hill smokes; 5. therefore this hill is fiery.

The second topic of the Nyáya proper is *Praméyá*, *i. e.*, the subjects of *Pramá*, or the subjects about which right knowledge is to be obtained. These are twelve: viz. 1. Soul (*átman*). 2. Body (*śaríra*). 3. Senses (*indriya*). 4. Objects of sense (*artha*). 5. Understanding or intellection (*buddhi*). 6. Mind (*manas*.) 7. Activity (*pravritti*). 8. Faults (*dosha*). 9. Transmigration (*pretyabháva*). 10. Consequences or fruits (*phala*). 11. Pain (*duḥkha*), 12. Emancipation (*apavarga*).

---

[1] *Hinduism Past and Present*, pp. 53-55. Abridged.

With regard to the fourteen other topics, they seem to be not so much philosophical categories as an enumeration of the regular stages through which a controversy is likely to pass. In India argument slides into wrangling disputation even more easily than in Europe, and the remaining topics certainly illustrate very curiously the captious propensities of a Hindu disputant, leading him to be quick in repartee, and ready with specious objections to the most conclusive argument.

There is first the state of *Saṁśaya*, or 'doubt about the point to be discussed.' Next, the *Prayojana*, or 'motive for discussing it.' Next follows a *Drishṭánta*, or, 'example' leading to the *Siddhánta*, or 'established conclusion.' Then comes an objector with his *Avayava*, or 'argument split up,' as we have seen, into five members. Next follows the *Tarka* or 'refutation,' (*reductio ad absurdum*) of his 'objection,' and the *Nirnaya*, or 'ascertainment of the true state of the case.' But this is not enough to satisfy a Hindu's passion for disputation. Every side of a question must be examined—every possible objection stated—and so a further *Váda*, or 'controversy' takes place, which of course leads to *Jalpa*, 'mere wrangling,' followed by *Vitaṇḍa*, 'cavilling;' *Hetv-ábhása*, 'fallacious reasoning;' *Chhala*, 'quibbling artifices;' *Játi* 'futile replies;' and *Nigrahasthána*, 'the putting an end to all discussion, by a demonstration of the objector's incapacity for argument.'

After enumerating these sixteen topics, Gautama proceeds to show how false notions are at the root of all misery. For from false notions comes the fault of liking or disliking, or being indifferent to anything; from that fault proceeds activity; from this mistaken activity proceed actions, involving either merit or demerit, which merit or demerit forces a man to pass through repeated births for the sake of its rewards or punishment. From these births proceeds misery, and it is the aim of philosophy to correct the false notions at the root of this misery.[1]

The name Iswara occurs once in the Sútras of Gautama, the founder of the Nyáya, but they say nothing of moral attributes as belonging to God, nor is His government of the world recognized. Nor can the system be said to believe in creation, inasmuch as it holds matter to be composed of eternal atoms. Confluent atoms, in themselves uncreated, composed the world. Soul, or rather spirit, is represented as multitudinous, and (like atoms) eternal. It is distinct from mind.[2]

2. The Vaiseshika.

The Vaiśeshika may be called a supplement of the Nyáya. It is attributed to a sage, nicknamed Kaṇáda (atom-eater). Colebrooke

[1] Abridged from *Hinduism*, by Monier Williams, pp. 187—190.
[2] Dr. Murray Mitchell, *Hinduism Past and Present*, pp. 56, 57.

explains Vaiśeshika as meaning "particular," as dealing with "particulars" or sensible objects. It begins by arranging its inquiries under seven *Padárthas*, or certain general properties or attributes that may be predicated of existing things.

The Vaiśeshika Sútras do not mention God. They go very fully into the doctrine of atoms—which, like the Nyáya, they declare to be uncaused and eternal. An atom is thus defined by Kanáda: "Something existing, without a cause, without beginning and end. It is contrary to what has a measure." Atoms are so exceedingly small that it requires three of them to be perceptible like a mote in a sunbeam.

It is held that the living individual souls of men (*jívátman*) are eternal, manifold, and *diffused everywhere throughout space*; so that a man's soul is as much in England as in Calcutta, though it can apprehend and feel and act only where the body happens to be.

The Vaiśeshika is dualistic in the sense of assuming the existence of *eternal atoms*, side by side either with *eternal souls*, or with the Supreme Soul of the universe.

The Vaiśeshika Aphorisms of Kanáda, with comments, have been translated by Mr. Gough, formerly Anglo-Sanskrit Professor in the 'Government College, Benares.'[1]

3. The Sánkhya.

The founder of this school is said to have been Kapila. In Gauḍapáda's commentary he is claimed to have been one of the seven Rishis, the "mind-born" sons of Brahmá. He was the irascible sage who reduced to ashes the 60,000 sons of King Sagara. Unlike the Nyáya, this is a *synthetic* system, as it were, placing things together. It is essentially dualistic. It holds that there are two primary eternal agencies. There is an eternally existing essence, called *Prakriti*, "that which produces or brings forth every thing else." This is sometimes, not very accurately, rendered by "*Nature.*"

Prakriti is variously called *Múla-prakriti*, 'root-principle;' *Amúlammúlam*, 'rootless root;' *Pradhána*, 'chief one;' *Avyakta*, 'unevolved evolver;' *Brahman*, 'supreme;' *Máyá*, 'power of illusion.' 'Producer, originator' would express the meaning more nearly than 'Nature.' From the absence of a root in the root, the root of all things is rootless.

Prakriti is supposed to be made up of three principles, called *Gunas*, or cords, supposed to bind the soul. They are *Sattva, Rajas, Tamas*; or Truth, Passion, and Darkness. These principles enter into all things; and on the relative quantity of each in any object depends the quality of the object.

---

[1] Published by Dr. J. Lazarus, Benares, Price, Rs. 4.

Souls (*Purush*) are countless in number; individual, sensitive, eternal, unchangeable. All that is done by Prakriti is done on behalf of soul. In its own nature soul is without qualities, until united with Prakriti. The union of the two is compared to a lame man mounted on a blind man's shoulder; the pair are then both (as it were) capable of perception and movement.

Beginning from the original rootless germ Prakriti, the Sánkhya counts up (*San-khyáti*) synthetically (whence its name of 'synthetic enumeration') twenty-three other Tattwas or entities—all productions of the first, and evolving themselves spontaneously out of it, as cream out of milk, or milk out of a cow,—while it carefully distinguishes them all from a twenty-fifth, *Purusha*, the soul, which is wholly in its own nature destitute of Gunas, though liable to be bound by the Gunas of Prakriti.

The process is thus stated in the Sánkhya-káriká: "The root and substance of all things (except soul) is Prakriti. It is no production. Seven things produced by it are also producers. Thence come sixteen productions (*vikára*). Soul, the twenty-fifth essence, is neither a production nor producer."

According to the Sánkhya system, the five grosser elements, (*mahábhúta*) with their distinguishing properties and corresponding organs of sense, are the following:

	Distinguishing Property.	Organ of Sense.
1. *Ákáśa*, ether	Sound	The Ear
2. *Váyu*, air	Tangibility	The Skin
3. *Tejas*, fire, light	Colour	The Eye
4. *Ápas*, water	Taste	The Tongue
5. *Prithiví*, earth	Smell	The Nose

There are eleven organs produced by *Ahankára*, the five organs of sense, ear, skin, eye, tongue, nose; and five organs of action, larynx (the throat), hand, foot, and excretory and generative organs, and an eleventh organ standing between them *viz.*, *Manas*, 'the mind' which is regarded as an internal organ of perception, volition, and action.

The liberation of *Purusha*, or soul, from the fetters which bind it in consequence of its union with Prakriti, is done by conveying the correct knowledge of the 24 constituent principles of creation; and rightly discriminating the soul from them.

In the Sánkhya there is no place for God; and accordingly it is known among Hindus by the name of Niríśwara Sánkhya, or the *Sánkhya without the Lord*.

The chief exponents of the system are the *Sánkhya Káriká* and the *Sánkhya Pravachana* or *Sútras*. The former has been translated into English by Mr. Davies; the latter by Dr. Ballantyne. The *Sánkhya Pravachana* consists of six books and 526 sútras.

4. The Yoga.

The Yoga, founded by Patanjali, is often styled the Theistic Sánkhya. It agrees in its general principles with the Sánkhya proper, but claims greater orthodoxy by directly acknowledging the existence of God. The Supreme Being of the Yoga is a soul distinct from other souls, unaffected by the ills with which they are beset; unconcerned with good or bad deeds and their consequences, "a spirit unaffected by works, having for one of his appellations the mystical monosyllable Om." Practically he is a nonentity, introduced to satisfy popular feeling, prejudiced against the Sánkhya as atheistic.

Indian philosophy makes salvation dependent upon right knowledge—that is the knowledge of the essential distinction between soul and non-soul. This right knowledge is generally supposed to be attainable only with the aid of the ascetic exercises prescribed in the Yoga Sástra.

The word *Yoga* now usually means *union;* and it is generally understood to teach how the human soul may attain complete union with the Supreme Soul. But Patanjali gives it a different meaning: "*Yoga* is the suppression of the transformations of the thinking principle." The mind is reduced to a state of vacuity, so that it ceases to act. The following are the exercises to be employed:—

1. *Yama,* restraint. 2. *Niyama,* religious observances. 3. *Ásana,* postures. 4. *Pránáyáma,* regulation of the breath. 5. *Pratyáhára,* restraint of the senses. 6. *Dhárana,* fixed attention. 7. *Dhyána,* contemplation. 8. *Samádhi,* profound meditation.

All wandering thoughts are to be called in, and attention fixed on some one object. Any object will answer if it is thought of alone; other thoughts must be suppressed. At last there is profound meditation without any object.

Great importance is attached to *ásana,* or postures. At an early period they were fixed as 84, but of this number ten are specially recommended. The following directions are given regarding some of them:

The Lotus Posture.—The right foot should be placed on the left thigh, and the left foot on the right thigh; the hands should be crossed, and the two great toes should be firmly held thereby; the chin should be bent down to the chest; and in this posture the eyes should be directed to the tip of the nose.

Gomukha, or Cow's Mouth Posture.—Put the right ankle on the left side of the chest, and similarly the left ankle on the right side.

Fowl Posture.—Having established the lotus posture, if the hand be passed between the thigh and the knees and placed on the earth so as to lift the body aloft, it will produce the fowl seat.

Bow Posture.—Hold the great toes with the hands and draw them to the ears as in drawing a bowstring.

The regulation of the breath, *pránáyáma*, is likewise of great importance. "The usual mode is after assuming the posture prescribed, to place the ring finger of the right hand on the left nostril, pressing it so as to close it, and to expire with the right; then to press the right nostril with the thumb, and to inspire through the left nostril, and then to close the two nostrils with the ring finger and the thumb, and to stop all breathing. The order is reversed in the next operation, and in the third act the first form is required."[1]

Marvellous powers are attributed to the man fully initiated in the Yoga. The past and present are unveiled to his gaze. He sees things invisible to others. He hears the sounds that are in distant worlds. He becomes stronger than the elephant, bolder than the lion, swifter than the wind. He mounts at pleasure into the air or dives into the depths of the earth and the ocean. He acquires mastery over all things, whether animated or inanimate.

The whole belief is a delusion. The brain is the organ of the mind. To enable it to act properly, it must have a good supply of pure blood. The blood is purified by fresh air entering into the lungs by breathing. From want of sufficient food and suppression of the breath, the blood of the Yogi is small in quantity and impure. The brain does not act properly. He may be in a dreamy condition or almost unconscious. Barth, a French writer, a distinguished Sanskrit scholar, says of the Yoga exercises: "Conscientiously observed, they can only issue in folly and idiocy."[2]

YOGA SASTRA, noticed below, contains a full account of the system, with numerous extracts from Patanjali's Sútras.[3]

5. MIMÁNSÁ.

This is sometimes called Púrva-Mímánsá, because founded on the Mantras and Bráhmanas, in contradistinction to the Uttara-Mímánsá or Vedánta, based on the later Upanishads.

Jaimini, its founder, did not deny the existence of God, but practically he makes the Veda the only God. The Veda, he says, is itself authority, and has no need of an authorizer. *Dharma* consists in the performance of the rites and sacrifices prescribed in the Veda, because they are so prescribed, without reference to the will or approval of any personal god, for Dharma is itself the bestower of reward.

Jaimini asserts the absolute eternity of the Veda, and he declares that only eternally pre-existing objects are mentioned in it. Another doctrine maintained by him is that sound is eternal, or rather, that an eternal sound underlies all temporary sound.[4]

---

[1] Quoted by Mr. R. C. Bose from the translation of the Yoga Shastra by Dr. Rajendralala Mitra. [2] *Religions of India*, p. 83. [3] 8vo. 78 pp. 2¼ As. Post-free, 3 As. Sold by Mr. A. T. Scott. [4] Abridged from Monier Williams. An excellent sketch of the different systems of philosophy is given in his *Hinduism*. S. P. C. K., 2s. 6d.

6. The Vedánta.

This system, though described last, has long been the chief philosophy of India. It is the truest exponent of the habits of thought of the Hindu mind. The term[1], says Colebrooke, "literally signifies, 'conclusion of the Veda,' and bears reference to the Upanishads, which are, for the most part, terminating sections of the Vedas to which they belong. It implies, however, the doctrine derived from them, and extends to books of sacred authority, in which that doctrine is thence deduced; and in this large acceptation, it is 'the end and scope of the Vedas."[2]

An explanation of the system is given in the following pages.

Eclectic School—The Bhagavad Gita.

Dr. Murray Mitchell gives the following sketch of the Bhagavad Gítá:

"Its great effort is to harmonise the doctrines of the Yoga, the Sánkhya, and the Vedánta. It begins by dwelling on the exceeding value of concentrating the mind, according to the first of these systems, and so attaining to union with Deity. Quiescence is essential; the sage must be absorbed in contemplation. While lauding the Yoga, the Gítá steers clear of the wild asceticism and magic that are the main characteristics of the system. The metaphysics of the Sánkhya as regards Purusha, Prakriti, &c., are adopted. But the doctrine of a Supreme Spirit as presiding over them is added—an alteration of a fundamental character. There are also said to be two kinds of Prakriti; which also is an essential change. . . . Finally Krishna reveals himself to Arjuna in his supreme form as possessed of countless faces, countless mouths, countless eyes—as, in fact, all things—and blazing like a thousand suns. This passage is a striking proof of the extravagance of the Hindu mind, which, in fact, can never discriminate between greatness and bigness, and totally lacks the taste for natural simplicity. The practical conclusion of the whole is that every man should strenuously perform the duties of his caste; and Arjuna, being a Kshatriya has nothing to do with whimpering; for fighting, killing, is his function. And so the warrior is convinced and plunges into the battle.

"The book is full of contradictions. Contemplative quietism is enjoined in one place; and in another energetic action. Further, the attempt to harmonize the three systems of philosophy ends in total failure. Two of them must be stripped of their distinctive features before even the semblance of unity can be secured. The 'Song' is mainly, though not wholly, Vedántist, that is pantheistic, in its doctrine."[3]

A complete English translation of the Bhagavad Gítá, with explanatory notes, and an examination of its doctrines, is sold at four annas by Mr. A. T. Scott.

---

[1] *Veda-anta*, end of the Veda.
[2] *Essays on the Philosophy of the Hindus.*
[3] *Hinduism Past and Present*, pp. 72-74 (slightly abridged.)

Vedantism, in its earlier form, as given in the VEDANTA-SUTRAS and its later form, in the VEDANTA-SARA, will now be described.

THE VEDANTA-SUTRAS.

Gough and Indian scholars generally claim to find traces of Vedántic doctrines in some of the later Vedic hymns; but all are agreed that the Upanishads form their foundation.

The meaning of *Upanishad* is disputed. According to Max Müller:

> "All we can say for the present is that Upanishad, besides being the recognized title of certain philosophical treatises, occurs also in the sense of doctrine and of secret doctrine, and that it seems to have assumed this meaning from having been used originally in the sense of session or assembly in which one or more pupils receive instruction from a teacher."[1]

They have been estimated at 170 in number, but new names are being added to the list. Max Müller says in his *History of Ancient Sanskrit Literature*:

> "During the latter ages of Indian history, when none of the ancient Upanishads could be found to suit the purpose, the founders of new sects had no scruple and no difficulty in composing new Upanishads of their own. This accounts for the large and evergrowing number of these treatises. Every new collection of MSS., every new list of Upanishads given by native writers, adds to the number of those which were known before; and the most modern compilations seem now to enjoy the same authority as the really genuine treatises."

Dr. Murray Mitchell says of the Upanishads:

> "These are by no means either systematic or homogeneous. They have well been called 'guesses at truth'; for they present no formal solution of great problems. They contradict one another; the same writer sometimes contradicts himself. They are often exceedingly obscure, and to Western minds repellent—vague, mystical, incomprehensible. A few rise to sublimity; others are nonsensical—'wild and whirling words,' and nothing more. Yet there is frequently earnestness —a groping after something felt to be needful; there is the yearning of hearts dissatisfied and empty. In this lies the value of the Upanishads."[2]

An attempt is made to systematise the teaching of the Upanishads in the *Vedánta-Sútras*, called also the *Brahma Sútras*, *Uttara Mímánsá Sútras*, and *Sáríraka Sútras*.

Authorship.—The *Vedánta-Sútras* are attributed to BÁDARÁYANA, supposed to be the same with *Vyása* or *Veda-Vyása*; also called

---

[1] *The Upanishads*, Vol. I. p. lxxxii. [2] *Hinduism Past and Present*, p. 4.

Krishna Dwaipáyana, Krishna island-born. According to mythology, he had in a former state, being then a Brahman, bearing the name of Apántara-Tamas, acquired a perfect knowledge of revelation and of the divinity, and was consequently qualified for eternal beatitude. Nevertheless, by special command of the deity, he resumed a corporeal frame and the human shape, at the period intervening between the third and fourth ages of the present world, and was compiler of the Vedas, as his title of Vyása implies."[1]

With the want of ability to weigh evidence characteristic of Hindus,[2] Vyása, besides arranging the Vedas, is generally believed to have written the Vedánta-Sútras, the Mahábhárata, and some of the principal Puránas. Books with such discordant opinions could not have proceeded from a single person. It was a common practice in India, to secure favourable notice of a work, to attribute it to some rishi. In South India there are treatises not more than one or two centuries old, which profess to have been written by Agastya!

Thibaut, referring to the Sútras of the two branches of the Mímánsá, says:—

"There can be no doubt that the composition of these two collections of Sútras was preceded by a long series of preparatory literary efforts of which they merely represent the highly condensed outcome. This is rendered probable by the analogy of other Sástras, as well as by the exhaustive thoroughness with which the Sútras perform their task of systematising the teaching of the Veda, and is further proved by the frequent references which the Sútras make to the views of earlier teachers."[3]

When Composed.—Thibaut says: "The time at which the two Mimánsá-Sútras were composed we are at present unable to fix with any certainty." But he adds: "It appears that already at a very early period the Vedánta-Sútras had come to be looked upon as an authoritative work, not to be neglected by any who wished to affiliate their own doctrines to the Veda."[3]

The references to the Yoga of Patanjali, the atheistical Sánkhya of Kapila, and the atomic system of Kanáda, show the Vedánta-Sútras to be posterior to them. "From this," says Colebrooke, "which is also supported by other reasons, there seems to be good ground for considering the Sáríraka to be the latest of the six grand systems of doctrine (darsana) in Indian philosophy."

Obscurity of the Vedanta-Sutras.—Thibaut says:

"All Sútras aim at conciseness; that is clearly the reason to which this whole species of literary composition owes its existence . . . At the same time the manifest intention of the Sútra writers is to express themselves

---

[1] Colebrooke's *Essays*. [2] See Dr. Bhandarkar's *Lecture on the Critical, Comparative, and Historical Method of Enquiry*. Bombay Nirnaya Sagar Press, 1888.

[3] Introduction to Translation of Vedánta-Sútras, pp. xi, xii. xiii, xvi.

with as much clearness as the consciseness affected by them admits of. . . . Hence the possibility of understanding without a commentary a very considerable portion at any rate of the ordinary Sútras. Altogether different is the case of the two Mimánsá Sútras. There scarcely one single Sútra is intelligible without a commentary. The most essential words are habitually dispensed with; nothing is, for instance, more common than the simple omission of the subject or predicate of a sentence. And when here and there a Sûtra occurs whose words construe without anything having to be supplied the phraseology is so eminently vague and obscure, that without the help derived from a commentary we should be unable to make out to what subject the Sútra refers."[1]

Colebrooke expresses the same opinion: "The *Sáríraka Sútras* are in the highest degree obscure, and could never have been intelligible without an ample interpretation."

As an illustration, the first four Sútras may be quoted, the translation giving the exact words in the original:

1. Then therefore the enquiry into Brahman.
2. From which the origin of this.
3. From its being the source of Scripture.
4. But that because it is connected as their purport.

Sankara's Commentary on the above occupies about 32 octavo pages; nearly three pages are devoted to "then."

Commentaries.—"Fitz-Edward Hall, in his Bibliographical Index, mentions 14 commentaries, copies of which had been inspected by himself. Some of them are indeed not commentaries in the strict sense of the word, but rather systematic expositions of the doctrine supposed to be propounded in the Sútras; but, on the other hand, there are in existence several true commentaries which had not been accessible to Fitz-Edward Hall."[2]

"Among ancient scholiasts of the Brahma-Sútras," says Colebrooke, "the name of Baudháyana occurs: an appellation to which reverence, as to that of a saint or *rishi*, attaches. He is likewise the reputed author of a treatise on law. An early gloss (commentary), under the designation of *Vritti*, is quoted without the author's name, and is understood to be adverted to in the remarks of later writers, in several instances, when no particular reference is however expressed. It is apparently Baudháyana's."[3]

Of all the commentaries the oldest extant and most celebrated, is that of Sankaráchárya, selected by Thibaut for translation. He says:

"The Sankara-bháshya is the authority most generally deferred to in India as to the right understanding of the Vedánta-Sútras, and ever since Sankara's time the majority of the best thinkers of India have been men belonging to his school."

---

[1] Introduction to translation of Vedánta-Sútras. pp. 14, 15.
[2] Thibaut, Introduction, p. xvi. [3] *Essays on the Philosophy of the Hindus.*

"But to the European a question will of course suggest itself at once, viz. whether or not Sankara's explanations faithfully render the intended meaning of the author of the Sútras?

"This is a task which would have to be undertaken even if Sankara's views as to the true meaning of the Sútras and Upanishads had never been called into doubt on Indian soil; but it becomes much more urgent, and at the same time more feasible when we meet in India itself with systems claiming to be Vedántic and based on interpretations of the Sútras and Upanishads more or less different from those of Sankara. The claims of those systems to be in possession of the right understanding of the fundamental authorities of the Vedánta must at any rate be examined, even if we should finally be compelled to reject them.

"The bháshya, which in this connexion is the first to press itself upon our attention, is the one composed by the famous Vaishnava theologian and philosopher, Rámánuja, who is supposed to have lived in the 12th century. The Rámánuja, or, as it is often called, the Srí-bháshya, appears to be the oldest commentary extant next to Sankara's. It is further to be noted that the sect of the Rámánujas occupies a pre-eminent position among the Vaishnava sects. The Srí-bháshya strikes one throughout as a very solid performance, due to a writer of extensive learning and great power of argumentation. Rámánuja also claims to follow in his bháshya the authority of Bodháyana."[1]

Thibaut shows, by quotations, "that the ancient teachers, the ripest outcome of whose speculations and discussions is embodied in the Vedánta-Sútras, disagreed among themselves on points of vital importance." . . . They show "that recognised authorities—deemed worthy of being quoted in the Sútras—denied that doctrine on which the whole system of Sankara hinges, *viz.*, the doctrine of the absolute identity of the individual soul with Brahman."[2]

Colebrooke mentions the following, in addition to Baudháyana and Rámánuja, as having written commentaries on the Sáríraka-Sútras, differing essentially on some points from Sankara's: Ballabha Achárya, Bhatta Bháscara, Ananta Tírtha, surnamed Madhu, and Nílakantha.

He adds: "These multiplied expositions of the text and of the gloss furnish an inexhaustible fund of controversial disquisition, suited to the disputatious schoolmen of India."[3]

Size and Divisions.—Colebrooke thus describes them:

"The Sútras of Bádaráyana are arranged in four books or lectures (*adhyáya*), each subdivided into four chapters or quarters (*páda*). They are distributed very unequally into sections, arguments, cases or topics (*adhikarana*). The entire number of Sútras is 555; of *adhikaranas*, 191. But in this there is a little uncertainty, for it appears from Sankara, that earlier commentaries subdivided some *adhikaranas*, where he writes the aphorisms in one section.

[1] Abridged from Thibaut's Introduction, pp. 14-17.
[2] Introduction, pp. xix, xx. [3] *Essay on Vedanta*.

"An *adhikarana* consists of five members or parts; 1st, the subject and matter to be explained; 2nd, the doubt or question concerning it; 3rd, the plausible solution or *primâ facie* argument; 4th, answer, or demonstrated conclusion and true solution; 5th, the pertinence or relevancy and connexion.

"But in Bádaráyana's aphorisms no *adhikarana* is fully set forth. Very frequently the solution only is given by a single sútra, which obscurely hints the question, and makes no allusion to any different plausible solution, nor to arguments in favour of it. More rarely the opposed solution is examined at some length, and arguments in support of it are discussed through a string of brief sentences."[1]

Contents.—The following summary is abridged from a very full analysis given by Thibaut in his Introduction. Thibaut compares the different explanations of Sútras given by Sankara and Rámánuja; but, as a rule, only the views of the former are mentioned in the following outline.

I. ADHYAYA.—The First Páda begins with laying down the fundamental positions with regard to Brahma; it is that from which the world originates, the source of the Vedas, the uniform topic of all Vedánta texts. It is shown that the cause of the world is an intelligent principle, and cannot be identified with the non-intelligent pradhána from which the world springs according to the Sánkhyas. The Second Páda shows that the being which consists of mind, whose body is breath, &c., is not the individual soul, but Brahma. The Sútras emphatically dwell on the difference of the individual soul and the highest Self, whence Sankara is obliged to add an explanation that the difference is to be understood as not real, but as due to false limiting adjuncts of the highest Self. The Third Páda shows that the Imperishable in which the ether is woven, the highest person who is to be meditated upon with the syllable Om, the small ether within the lotus of the heart, &c., is Brahma. The gods are capable of the knowledge of Brahma, but Súdras are altogether disqualified. The last Páda is specially directed against the Sánkhyas. Brahma is held to be not only the efficient cause of the world, but its material cause as well. The world springs from Brahma by way of modification (*parínáma*). The refutation of the Sánkhya views is applicable to other theories also, such as the doctrine of the world having originated from atoms.

II. ADHYAYA.—The First Páda shows that Brahma, although of the nature of intelligence, may yet be the cause of the non-intelligent material world, and that it is not contaminated by the qualities of the world when the latter is refunded into Brahma. Like does not always spring from like. Brahma, though destitute of material and instruments of action, may yet produce the world just as the gods by their mere power create palaces, &c., and as milk by itself turns into curds; Brahma, although emitting the world

[1] *Essay on the Vedánta.*

from itself, remains one and undivided; Brahma is able to create the world by means of the manifold powers which it possesses. Brahma, in creating the world, has no motive, but follows a sportive impulse. Brahma is justified from the charges of partiality and cruelty from the inequalities of life as it acts with a view to the merit and demerit of individual souls. The Second Páda refutes by arguments independent of Vedic passages the more important philosophical theories concerning the origin of the world which are opposed to the Vedánta view. It is shown that a non-intelligent first cause, such as the pradhána of the Sánkhyas, is unable to create and dispose; the Váiseshika doctrine is refuted that the world originates from atoms set in motion by *Adrishta.* Various schools of Bauddha philosophers are impugned. The last part refers to the doctrine of the Bhágavatas, the forerunners of Rámánuja. The Third Páda discusses the question whether the different forms of existence which, in their totality, constitute the world, have an origin or not, *i.e.,* whether they are co-eternal with Brahma or issue from it and are refunded into it at stated intervals. The first part treats of the five elementary substances. Ether is not co-eternal with Brahma, but springs from it as its first effect; air springs from ether, fire from air, water from fire, earth from water. The reabsorption takes place in the inverse order of the emission. The remainder of the Páda is taken up by a discussion of the nature of the individual soul. It is held to be eternal, and therefore not produced like the elements. The question is discussed whether the soul is of very minute size or all-pervading. Sútra 43 declares that the soul is a part (*amśa*) of Brahma, but Sankara holds that is only "as it were," the one universal indivisible Brahma having no real parts, but appearing to be divided owing to its limiting adjuncts. Rámánuja holds that the souls are in reality parts of Brahma. The Fourth Páda treats of the Pránas, 11 in number, and of minute size. They sprung from Brahma and are guided by special divinities. The evolution of names and forms is the work of the highest Lord.

III. Adhyaya.—The First Páda treats of what happens to the soul after death, and discusses the fate of those who go to the moon and those whose good works do not entitle them to that privilege. The descent from the moon is very rapid; souls which finally enter plants do not participate in their life, but are merely in external contact with them. The Second Páda treats of the soul in a dreaming state; in deep dreamless sleep the soul abides within Brahma in the heart; in a swoon there is half union; the nature of the highest Brahma in which the individual soul is merged in the state of deep sleep is discussed; Brahma is held to be in reality void of all distinctive attributes which are altogether due to the *Upádhis*; lastly it is held, in opposition to Jaimini, that the reward of works is allotted by the Lord. The Third Páda describes how the individual soul is enabled by meditation on Brahma to obtain final release. The question is considered whether in all the meditations on Brahma all its qualities are to be included or only those mentioned in the special *vidyá*. It is asserted that a man dying possessed of true knowledge shakes off all his good and evil deeds,[1] the former passing to his friends, the latter to his enemies. The Fourth Páda proves that the knowledge of Brahma is not subordinate to action, but independent; from ascetics no actions but only knowledge is required. Nevertheless the actions enjoined by Scripture, as sacrifices, &c., are required as conducive to the rise of *vidyá* in the mind. Certain relaxations allowed of the laws regarding food, are meant only for cases of extreme need. The duties of the four stages are obligatory on him who does not strive after *mukti*. Some of the results of *vidyá* are described.

IV. Adhyaya:—The First Páda gives rules for meditation on the Átman. It is not an act to be accomplished once only, but is to be repeated again and again. The Átman is to be viewed as constituting one's own Self; meditation is to be carried on in a sitting posture at any time, and in any favourable place, and to be continued until death. When through these meditations the knowledge of Brahma has been reached, the *vidván* is no longer affected by the consequences of either past or future evil deeds; but this does not extend to works on which the present existence of the devotee depends. When the latter have been fully worked out, the *vidván* becomes united with Brahma. The Second Páda and the two remaining describe the fate of the *vidván* after death. In explaining the Sútras, Sankara and Rámánuja generally differ widely. Only the explanations of the former will be noticed. On the death of the *vidván* who possesses the lower knowledge, his senses are merged in the *manas*, the *manas* in the *prána*, the *prána* in the *jíva*, the *jíva* in the subtile elements. On the death of him who possesses the higher knowledge, his *pránas*, elements, &c., are merged in Brahma, so as to be no longer distinct in any way. The *vidván* leaves the body by the artery called *sushumná*, the *avidván* by another one. The departing soul passes up to the sun by a ray of light what exists at night as well as during day. The Third Páda reconciles the different accounts given in the Upanishads as to the stations of the way which leads the *vidván* up to Brahma. By the 'stations' are to be understood, not only the subdivisions of the way, but also the divine beings which lead the soul on.

The Brahma to which the departed soul is led by the guardians of the path of the gods is not the highest Brahma; but the *Saguna* Brahma. Those only are guided to Brahma who have not worship-

[1] The illustrations given in the commentary are "Shaking off all evil as a horse shakes his hair, and shaking off the body as the moon frees herself from the mouth of Rahu." Thibaut, Vol. II, p. 225.

ped it under a symbolic form. The Fourth Páda teaches that when, on his death, the soul of the owner of the highest knowledge obtains final release, it does not acquire any new characteristics, but merely manifests itself in its true nature. The relation of the released soul to Brahma means absolute non-separation, identity. The released are embodied or disembodied according to their wish. The soul of the released can animate several bodies at the same time, as the same lamp may have several wicks. The released souls participate in all the perfections and powers of Brahma, with the exception of the power of creating and sustaining the world. They do not return to new forms of embodied existence.

Thibaut, when contrasting the opinions of Sankara and Rámánuja generally accepts the latter as the more reasonable. In the examination of Vedánta doctrines, there will be numerous references to the Vedánta-Sútras.

A full and accurate account of the Vedánta is given in Colebrooke's Essays.

The more modern form of Vedántism will now be described.

VEDANTA-SARA.

INTRODUCTION.

The Vedanta-Sara, 'Essence of the Vedánta,' says Colebrooke, "is a popular compendium of the entire doctrine of the Vedánta. It is the work of Sadánanda, disciple of Advayánanda or Advaitánanda, and has become the text for several commentaries, among the rest the *Vidvanmanó-ranjini*, 'Rejoicer of the Mind of the Learned,' by Rama-tírtha, and the *Subódhini*, by Nrisimha Sarasvati, disciple of Krishnánanda."

The Vedánta-Sára is held in esteem as a correct exponent of orthodox Vedántism. Ballantyne says that it is "the compendium in which this doctrine is usually first studied."

Nothing seems to be known of the author. Though the time of its composition cannot be fixed definitely, it is known to be comparatively modern. Professor Venis, in the Preface to his translation of the Vedántic *Siddhánta muktavali* of Prakásananda, says:

> "The exact date of the *Siddhánta muktavali* is unknown. The work may however be assigned with some probability to the last quarter of the sixteenth century; for it is referred to by Appaya-dikshiti, who had reached a good old age in 1626 A.D., and who (it would appear from the evidence now available) was contemporary with Prakásananda." p. iii.

Colonel Jacob, the latest translator of the Vedánta-Sára, considers that it was composed shortly after the above work.

There are three English translations. The first, by Dr. Roer, was published in the Journal of the Bengal Asiatic Society in 1845. A greatly improved translation was incorporated by Dr. J. R. Ballantyne, Principal of the Sanskrit College, Benares, in a lecture on the Vedánta delivered in 1850. A third translation, by Colonel G. A. Jacob, was published in 1881. The third edition, revised, appeared in 1891.[1] Besides being an improved translation, it contains copious valuable annotations. The following translation is from Ballantyne; but, here and there, important clearer renderings are given from Colonel Jacob. Colonel Jacob has also published the Vedánta-Sára in Sanskrit with the commentaries of Nrisimhasarasvatí and Rámatírtha, with Notes and Indices.[2]

The latest phase of Vedántism is found also in another standard treatise, probably posterior to the Vedánta-Sára, called the *Vedánta Paribháshá*. It has been translated by Professor Venis, and published in *The Pandit* for 1882-85. Numerous extracts from it are given by Nehemiah Goreh in his *Refutation of Hindu Philosophical Systems.*

The Vedánta-Sára is continuous; but, for greater clearness, Colonel Jacob has divided his translation into fourteen sections, adopted below, to which a brief summary has been added.

I. Introductory stanzas.

II. The Qualifications necessary in a student of the Vedánta; the Subject-Matter; the Connection between the subject-matter and the treatise; the Advantages of the Study.

III. Erroneous Imputation; the 'Real' and the 'Unreal', Brahma and Ignorance.

IV. Collective and Distributive Ignorance, I'śvara and Prájna identical; the 'Fourth'; the two powers of Ignorance,—Envelopment and Projection.

V. The Causal, Subtile and Gross Bodies, with which Brahma is illusorily associated; the 'Fourth State.'

VI. Meaning of the sentence, 'Truly all this is Brahma'; Refutation of Chárváka, Bauddha, and other fallacies.

VII. Meaning of 'Refutation'; the phenomenal world only the illusory effect of Brahma, who is its illusory material cause.

VIII. Meaning of 'That' and 'Thou' in the great sentence determined by erroneous Imputation and its Refutation.

IX. Explanations of the Great Sentence, 'That art Thou;' the three Relations.

X. Erroneous explanations of the Great Sentence; the true meaning.

---

[1] It appeared in Trübner's *Oriental Series*, entitled *A Manual of Hindu Pantheism*. It is now published by Kegan Paul, Trench, Trübner & Co., Price 5s.

[2] Printed and Published by Tukárám Jávají, Nirnaya Sagar Press, Bombay. Price Re. 1½.

XI. Meaning of the sentence, 'I am Brahma'; he who understands the Great Sentence realises his union with It.

XII. Means to be employed to realize the Great Sentence.

XIII. The eight Means subservient to Meditation without distinction of Subject and Object.

XIV. Characteristics of the Jívanmukta.

TRANSLATION

OF

THE VEDANTA-SARA.

I.

(INTRODUCTION.)

Salutation to Ganesa!

For the accomplishment of what is desired, I take refuge with the Indivisible (*akhanda*), (that consists of)[1] existence, knowledge, and joy,—no object fitted for the organ of voice (to declare), nor for the mind (to comprehend)—*Soul*—the substrate[2] of all.

Having reverenced my preceptor, Advayánanda, who is significantly so named (undivided joy)—because the notion of duality is (in his case) destroyed—I shall, according to my understanding of it, declare the Essence of the Vedánta.

(But what is meant by the term) Vedánta? (By this is meant) the evidence (of there being nothing but Brahma) constituted by the Upanishads, and (by the same term are denoted) such works ancillary thereto, as the Sárírika Sútras.

II.

(THE QUALIFICATIONS NECESSARY IN A STUDENT OF THE VEDANTA; THE SUBJECT-MATTER; THE CONNECTION BETWEEN THE SUBJECT-MATTER AND THE TREATISE; THE ADVANTAGES OF THE STUDY.)

Since, in consequence of this work being concerned about the Vedánta, it is clear that this has the same moving considerations (*anubandha*)[3] as that has, these do not require to be considered as if they were something different (from what the readers of the Vedánta are accustomed to).

In that (the Vedánta—what are) the moving considerations?[4] (They are) (1) The competent person (*adhikárin*), (2) The object-

---

[1] English words, enclosed within brackets, are added to complete the sense.

[2] That which is spread under. The substance supposed to furnish the basis in which the perceptible qualities inhere.

[3] Things previously known in order to understand other things.

[4] "Moving considerations." Col. Jacob says: "Various readings of this technical term have been proposed, such as 'motives,' *præcognita*, (things needful to be known before), &c. A lucid explanation of it is given by Dr. Ballantyne in his

matter (*vishaya*), (3) The relation (*sambandha*), and (4) The purpose (*prayojana*).

I. The '*competent person*' is that well-regulated person who, by the perusal, as prescribed, of the Vedas and their dependent sciences, has attained to a rough notion[1] of the sense of the whole Veda:—who, by renouncing, in this or in a former life, things desirable and things forbidden; and by observance of the constant and of the occasional ceremonies, of penances, and of devotions, being freed from all sin, is thoroughly purified in his heart, and who is possessed of the four requisites, (hereafter mentioned).

'*Things desirable*' are the means, such as the *jyotishṭoma*[2] sacrifice, of obtaining things desired—such as heaven.

'*Things forbidden*,' such as the killing of a Bráhman, are what lead to things undesired—such as hell.

'*Constant ceremonies*,' (*nitya*), such as the morning and evening prayers,[3] &c., are those which, in their omission (under any circumstances) are causes of sin.

'*Occasional ceremonies* (*naimittika*), such as the *játeshti*,[4] are those contingent on some occasion, such as the birth of a son.

'*Penances*' (*práyaschitta*), such as the *Chándráyana*,[5] are what cause (not the acquisition of anything positive, but) merely the removal of sin.

'*Devotions*' (*upásana*), such as (are inculcated in) the doctrine of the saint *Sándilya*[6], consist of mental operations whose object is Brahma with qualities.

Of these (three sets) of which the 'constant ceremonies' are the first, the chief purpose is the purification of the intellect; but of the 'devotions' the chief purpose is the concentration of it.

(The positions above laid down are deduced) from such scriptural texts as this, that "Him do the Brahmans seek to know by means of sacrifices (performed) in conformity with (the direc-

article entitled, *The Gist of the Vedánta as a Philosophy* (*Pandit*, for July 1867), and is as follows: 'With reference to the commencing of any scientific work, according to Hindu opinion, four questions present themselves—(1) what qualifications are required to render one competent to enter upon the study?—(2) what is the subject-matter?—(3) what connexion is there between the subject-matter and the book itself?—and (4) what inducement is there to enter upon the study at all? The answer to each of these questions is called an *anubandha*—a 'bond of connection' or 'cause'—because, unless a man knows what a given book is about, and whether he is competent to understand it, and what good the knowledge will do him, he cannot be expected to apply himself to the study of the book.'" Sanskrit Ed. of *Vedánta-Sára*, p. 168.

[1] "General idea." Col. Jacob. [2] Seven sacrifices of which Agnishtoma was the first. On the last day the squeezing, offering and drinking of the Soma juice took place. It was considered the holiest of all Brahmanical services. [3] The repetition of the *Gáyatri*, 5, 10, 28 or 100 times. [4] Birth-sacrifice. [5] Increasing or diminishing food by one mouthful daily during the light and dark fortnights of the moon. [6] The doctrine ascribed to the sage Sándilya.

tions of) the Veda";[1] and (they are deduced also) from such regulations as this that "By austerities one destroys sin[2]—by knowledge one obtains the water of immortality."

The result attendant on the constant and occasional ceremonies, and on devotion, is the attaining to the abode of the progenitors and of the celestials—(and this is deduced) from the text, "The abode of the progenitors is (to be attained to) by works, and the abode of the gods by knowledge."[3]

'Requisites' (*sádhana*) are (1) the discrimination of eternal substance from the transient; (2) disregard of the enjoyment of the fruits of here and hereafter; (3) the possession of tranquillity and self-restraint; and (4) desire of liberation.

(1.) 'Discrimination of the eternal substance from the transient,' is the discerning that Brahma is the eternal substance, and that all else is non-eternal.

(2.) 'Disregard of the enjoyment of the fruits of here and hereafter' is the entire neglect of them, because of the fact that the enjoyments of the things of hereafter, also, such as the water of immortality, are un-eternal, just as the enjoyments of the things of the present, such as garlands and unguents are un-eternal, because they are produced by works.

(3.) 'Tranquillity, Self-restraint,' &c., are (1) Tranquillity, (2) self-restraint, (3) quiescence, (4) endurance, (5) contemplation, and (6) faith.

a. 'Tranquillity' is the restraining of (the internal organ) the mind from objects different from the hearing, &c. (about Isvara.)

b. 'Self-Restraint' is the restraining of the *external* organs from objects different therefrom.

c. 'Quiescence' is the inaction of the organs thus restrained from objects different therefrom. Or—it is the abandonment, according to the injunction, of works enjoined.

d. 'Endurance' is the sustaining of such pairs as cold and heat (with indifference alike for the pain or pleasure they may tend to produce.)

e. 'Contemplation' (*samádhána*) is the intentness of the mind restrained (from all else) on the hearing, &c., (concerning the Lord) or on kindred objects.

f. 'Faith' (*sraddhá*) is belief in the assertions of the spiritual guide and of the Vedánta.

(4.) 'Desire of liberation' is the wish to be liberated.

Such a well-regulated person is a competent person (to engage in the study of the Vedánta).

---

[1] *Brihadáranyaka*, 4. 4, 22. [2] *Manu*, xii. 104. [3] *Brihad.* i. 5, 16.

(That such is the character of a fit enquirer may be inferred) from the scriptural text beginning, "Tranquil and self-restrained,[1] &c." And it has been said, "To him who is tranquil in mind, who has his organs in subjection, whose sins have disappeared, who acts according to the commandments, who is possessed of good qualities, docile, ever desiring liberation—this (doctrine of the Vedánta) is always proper to be imparted."[2]

II. The '*Object-matter*' (*vishaya*), is the fact—to be known for certain—that the soul and Brahma are one; for this is the drift of all Vedánta treatises.

III. The '*Relation*' (*sambandha*). This, between the identity (of Soul and Brahma) which is to be known as certain, and the evidence thereof contained in the scriptural treatises which ascertain it, is that of the information (communicated) and the informer.

IV. The '*End*' (*prayojana*) is the cessation of the ignorance which invades this identity that is to be known (of Soul and Brahma) and the attainment (by Soul, thereon) of that bliss which is his essence.

(This may be inferred) from the scriptural text, that "He who knows what Soul is, gets beyond grief;"[3] and from the text, that, "He who knows Brahma becomes Brahma."[4].

This qualified person being burned by the fire of this world in the shape of birth, death, and the like, as one whose head is heated (takes refuge) in a body of water, having approached, with tribute in his hands, a teacher who knows the Vedas, and who is intent on Brahma, follows him; for (there is) the Scriptural text, 'With fuel in his hands (as an offering, the enquirer approaches) him who knows the Vedas and is intent on Brahma, &c."[5]

The teacher, with the greatest kindness, instructs him by the method of the 'Refutation of erroneous Imputation;' (as might be inferred) from such texts as the one beginning, "To him, when he had approached, the learned man thus spoke, &c."[6]

III.

(Erroneous Imputation; the 'Real' and the 'Unreal'; Brahma and Ignorance.)

'Erroneous Imputation'[7] (*adhyáropa*) is the allegation that the Unreal is the Real—like the judgment, in respect of a rope which is no serpent, that it is a serpent.

---

[1] *Brihadáranyaka.* 4. 4. 26. [2] *Upadesasáhasrí*, 324. [3] *Chhándogya*, 7, 1. 3.
[4] *Muṇḍaka*, 3. 2. 9. [5] *Muṇḍaka*, i. 2. 12. [6] *Muṇḍaka*, i. 2. 13.

[7] Rendered by Col. Jacob, "Illusory Attribution." "In order to describe the pure abstraction Brahma, the teacher attributes to him, or superimposes on him, certain qualities which in reality do not belong to him, and then afterwards withdrawing them teaches that the residuum is the undifferenced Absolute."—Jacob, p. 42.

The 'Real' (*vastu*) is Brahma, existence, knowledge, and happiness, without a second. The 'Unreal' (*avastu*) is the whole aggregate of the senseless—beginning with Ignorance.

'Ignorance.' They (the Vedántins) declare that this is a somewhat that is not be called positively either entity or non-entity[1]—not a mere negation (but) the opponent of knowledge,—consisting of the three fetters.

(That there is such a thing as Ignorance may be deduced) from the consciousness of every man of being ignorant, and from such scriptural texts beginning with, "The power of the divine soul clothed with its qualities." &c.[2]

IV.

(Collective and Distributive Ignorance; I'śvara and Prájna identical; the 'Fourth'; the two Powers of Ignorance—Envelopment and Projection.)

This Ignorance is treated as one or as many accordingly as it is regarded collectively or distributively.[3] That is to say—as of trees, when regarded as a collection, the singular denomination is 'forest'—or, as of waters, when regarded as a collection, it (the singular denomination) is 'a lake,'—so the ignorances, attached to souls and apparently multitudinous, receive, when regarded as a collection, the singular denomination thereof (the name of 'Ignorance' in the singular.)

(That it is proper to speak of Ignorance as *one*, may be deduced) from such scriptural texts (as that which speaks of it) as "The unborn, the single, &c."[4]

This aggregation (of Ignorance), since it is the abode of its superior,[5] has chiefly pure goodness in it. Intellect (*chaitanya*) of which this is the abode being possessed of such qualities as omniscience, omnipotence, superintendence over all, imperceptible, all-pervading, Maker of the world, is called Isvara.

His omniscience (may be inferred) from the fact that he is the enlightener of all Ignorance; and from such scriptural texts as, "Who is omniscient—who knoweth all."[6]

This aggregation (of Ignorance), since it is the cause of all, is Isvara's causal body.[7] Since there is in it a plenitude of happiness, and it envelopes all as the cocoon (of the silkworm does its tenant); it is this that is called the sheath of happiness. This (body of the

[1] Existence or non-existence. If the world were allowed really to exist, dualism would follow. On the other hand it cannot be said to be absolutely non-existent, for it has an appearance as in a dream. [2] *Svetásvatara*, i. 3. [3] Taken together or singularly. [4] *Svetásvatara*, iv. 5. [5] "Having as its associate (*upádhi*) that which is most excellent." Jacob. [6] *Muṇḍuka*, i. 1. 9. [7] "As illusion overlying Brahma is the cause of the production of all things, it is called Isvara's causal or all-originating body." Jacob, p. 10.

deity) is (nothing different from) profound sleep, for it is into this that every soul (in profound sleep) subsides. Hence it is called the place of the dissolution of both the gross and subtile world.[1]

As a forest, when regarded distributively, takes the plural denomination 'trees'—or as a lake, when regarded distributively, takes that of 'waters,' so Ignorance, when regarded distributively, receives the plural name (Ignorances.) (This follows) from such scriptural texts as "Indra, by his powers, appears manifold."[2]

"Ignorance is regarded collectively or distributively according as it is viewed as a whole or as separate parts."[3]

Distributive Ignorance, since it is the abode of its Inferior (the human soul), has chiefly impure goodness in it. Intelligence located in this, having such qualities as want of knowledge and want of power, is called, the very defective intelligence, (*prájna*).[4] The smallness of its intelligence (may be inferred) from the fact that it is the illuminator of (but) one Ignorance. It has not the power of illuminating much, because its abode is not clear (being tainted by Passion and Darkness).

Since (Distributive Ignorance) is the cause of the conceit of individuality[5] and the like, it is (spoken of as) the individual's causal body. Since there is in it a plenitude of happiness, it (also) is called the sheath of happiness. It is (nothing different from) profound sleep, for it is in this that all ceases to do aught. Hence it (also) is called the place of the dissolution of both the gross and subtile body. At that time (during dreamless sleep) both Isvara and Prájna enjoy blessedness by means of the very subtile modifications of Ignorance, illumined by intellect. As the Scriptures say, "Prájna (the individual intelligence) enjoys bliss[6] (during dreamless sleep) being (then) more peculiarly that intelligence (which unfettered altogether, is joy simply). (It may also be inferred) from the fact that one in rising says, "I slept pleasantly,—I knew nothing."

Between these two, Ignorance regarded collectively and distributively, there is no difference, as there is none between a forest and its trees, or between a lake and its waters.

There is likewise no difference between Isvara and Prájna affected by these (two kinds of really identical Ignorance) as there is none between the ethereal space that is occupied by the forest and by the trees (that constitute the forest), or between the ethereal expanse that is reflected in the lake and in the waters thereof. (This may be inferred) from such texts as, "This Prájna is none other than the omniscient."[7]

---

[1] "When a man falls into a profound sleep, the external world and the world of dreams both cease to exist for him and then his position is held to be that described above." Ballantyne.

[2] Rig-Veda, 6, 47. 18. [3] Jacob. [4] *Prájna*, means intelligent. Applied here to an individual it is said to denote defective or limited intelligence, but in the Mándúkya Upan. 6, it is described as 'omniscient.' [5] "Cause of the making of 'I.'" *Jacob.* [6] *Mándúkya*, 5. [7] *Mándúkya*, 6.

As there is for the forest and its trees and for the ethereal space occupied by these, or for the lake and its waters, and for the ethereal expanse that is reflected therein, an absolute expanse in which these are located, so for these "two Ignorances and for Intelligence associated with them,"[1] there is an absolute intelligence which is their basis. This is called "the Fourth,"[2] as it is said in such texts as, "They regard him as blessed, tranquil, without duality, the Fourth."[3]

This one, the Fourth, pure intelligence, when not discriminated[4] apart from Ignorance and the intelligence located therein, like (the fire and the iron viewed indiscriminately in) an ignited iron ball, is what is the express meaning of (the term Thou in) the great sentence (That art Thou—meaning "Thou art Brahma"). But when discriminated, it is called the meaning indicated.[5]

This Ignorance has two powers—*envelopment* (*ávarana*) and *projection* (*vikshepa*).

As even a small cloud, by obstructing the path of the eye of the spectator, hides the sun's disc which extends over many leagues, such also is the enveloping power of Ignorance, which, though finite, by obstructing the mind of the observer, hides as it were the Soul which is infinite and not subject to worldly vicissitude. Thus it is said, "As the very stupid man, whose eye is covered by a cloud, thinks that the sun is covered by a cloud and void of radiance, so that (Soul) which, in the sight of the stupid, is as it were bound, that, in the shape of the eternal understanding, am I myself."[6]

In the Soul enveloped with this, there arises the impression that it is liable to worldly vicissitude—that it is an agent, a patient, happy, grieved, and so forth; as in the case of a rope concealed by ignorance in regard to its character (there arises) the impression that it is a snake.

The *projective* power is such that as ignorance regarding a rope produces by its own power on the rope enveloped by it (the appearance of) a snake or the like, so (this projective) Ignorance, by its own power raises up, on the soul enveloped by it (the appearance of) a world, ether, &c., (and thus the thinker mistakes *himself* for a mere mortal, as he mistook the rope for a snake.) Thus it is said, "The projective power can create (everything)

---

[1] Improved rendering from Jacob.

[2] There are four conditions of the soul, viz., (1) waking, (2) dreaming, (3) dreamless sleep; and (4) that which is here called "the fourth." Ballantyne.

[3] *Mándúkya*, 7. [4] Distinguished. [5] Ballantyne, in his translation of *Sáhityadarpana*, quoted by Jacob, says: "The meaning (that may belong to a word, is held to be three fold, namely Express, Indicated, and Suggested. The Express meaning is that conveyed to the understanding by the (word's) Denotation; The (meaning) Indicated is held to be conveyed by the (word's) suggestion. Let these be the three powers of a word." People say 'the hot iron burns the hand," meaning that the *heat* in the iron burns the hand. This is the meaning *indicated*. Thus in the great sentence "That art Thou," the meaning is "Thou, *apart* from the ignorance that now envelops thee, art That." Ballantyne abridged. [6] *Hastámalika*, 10.

beginning with the subtile body, and ending with the whole external universe."[1]

Intellect (*chaitanya*) located in Ignorance with its two powers (envelopment and projection) is in its own right the instrumental cause; and in virtue of what it is located in (Ignorance) the material cause (of all)—as the spider is personally the instrument and in virtue of its own body the material cause of its web.[2]

V.

(THE CAUSAL, SUBTILE AND GROSS BODIES WITH WHICH BRAHMA IS ILLUSORILY ASSOCIATED; THE FOURTH STATE.)

From Intellect immersed in Ignorance with the projective power in which *tamas* prevails, there arises the Ether:—from the Ether, Air; from Air, Fire; from Fire, Water; from Water, Earth. (This may be inferred) from such texts of Scripture as "From that (Intellect) from this same self was the Ether produced, &c."[3] That there is the prevalence of *tamas* in the cause of these (five elements—may be inferred) from the excess of senselessness observed in them, (—the elements being unenlightened by Intellect which they quite obscure).

Then (although darkness is the chief ingredient in the cause of these, yet as it is not the sole one, therefore) Purity, Foulness, and Darkness are produced in these (elemental products) Ether, &c., in the degree in which they exist in the cause.

It is these same (five) that are called also the 'subtile elements,' (*súkshamabhúta*), the 'that merely' (*tan-mátra*) and the 'not (yet) made into the (gross) five' (*a-panchíkrita*) (by intermixture).

From these (subtile elements) are produced the subtile bodies and the gross elements (*sthúla-bhútáni*) (afterwards explained).

The '*subtile bodies*' are the bodies whereby (the individuated Soul) is recognised (*linga-sarira*), consisting of the seventeen members.

The '*members*' are the set of five organs of sense, understanding and mind, the set of five organs of action and the five vital airs.

The '*organs of sense*' are those called the hearing, the touch, the sight, the taste, and the smell. These are produced from the separate *pure* particles of the Ether, &c., severally in their order.[4]

'*Understanding*'[5] (*buddhi*) is that condition of the internal instrument (*antah-karana*, the 'inner man)', which consists in assur-

---

[1] *Vákyasudhá*, v. 13.

[2] Brahma, regarded as pure spirit, is the *instrumental* cause, but not the *material* cause of the world. He is the material cause in virtue only of *that wherewith he hath invested himself*, which some people call 'matter,' and regard as really existing and which the Vedántins prefer calling 'Ignorance,'—denying its right to be regarded as really existing. Ballantyne.

[3] *Táittírya Upan.* ii. 1.

[4] The organ of hearing is produced from pure etherial particles, that of feeling from pure aerial particles, that of sight from light, taste from water, and smell from earth. Ballantyne. [5] Or Intellect.

ance. '*Mind*' (*manas*) is that condition of the inner man which consists in doubting or judging. In these two are included thinking and self-consciousness (or egoism). These are produced from the *mingled* pure portions belonging to the Ether, &c. That they are formed from the *pure* (*sáttwika*) particles (is evident) from their being luminous.

This understanding, being associated with the organs of sense, is the 'intelligent sheath' (*vijnánamaya-kosha*) (of the soul).[1] This, practically regarded, haunting this world or the other world, through its having the conceit that it is an agent and a patient, is called the 'inferior[2] soul' (*jíva*).

The mind, associated with the organs of action,[3] becomes the 'mental sheath', (*manomaya-kosha*).[4]

The '*organs of action*' are the voice, the hands, the feet, the organs of excretion, and generation. These again, severally in their order, are produced from the energetic particles of the Ether, &c., separately.

The '*vital airs*' are respiration (*prána*), flatulence (*vyána*), inspiration (*upána*), expiration (*udána*), and assimilation (*samána*). '*Respiration*' is that which goes forward, having its place in the fore part of the nose. '*Flatulence*,' which goes downwards, has its place in the lower intestine, &c. '*Inspiration*,' which goes everywhere, is found in the whole body. '*Expiration*,' having its place in the throat, is the ascending air that goes upwards. '*Assimilation*,' moving in the middle of the body, assimilates the food that is eaten or drunk.

Some say there are five other airs, named *Nága, Kúrma, Krikala, Devadatta* and *Dhananjaya*. '*Nága*' is that which causes belching; '*Kúrma*' produces winking, '*krikala*' produces hunger, '*Devadatta*,' yawning; '*Dhananjaya*,' nourishes.[5]

Others (the Vedantins) say that there are only five, because these are included under respiration and the rest.

This set of five vital airs (respiration, &c.) is produced from the mingled energetic particles that belong to the Ether, &c. This set of five, associated with the organs of action, becomes the '*respiratory* sheath' (*pránamaya-kosha*). That this (set) is a

---

[1] The individual Soul is regarded as deposited in a succession of sheaths, enveloping one another like the coats of an onion. The first, or innermost, is the one just described. The outmost sheath is our body of flesh and blood. The intermediate ones will be described in their order. Ballantyne.

[2] The Sanskrit word (*Vyávahárika*) here means rather 'belonging to the everyday life,—conventional,—practical.' Jacob.

[3] In his edition of the *Sanskrit* text, Col. Jacob has shown that the reading here should rather be 'organs of sense.' See his note on p. 177 of that work.

[4] The soul (*jíva*) was divided from Brahma, first by the conceit of its own individuality. It is removed a step further by the operations of thinking and doubting. Ballantyne.

[5] Some others are the followers of Kapila. Ballantyne translates the airs as the snake, the tortoise, the partridge, the conch of Arjuna, and the god of fire.

5

product of the energetic particles (is evident) from the fact that it consists of action.[1]

Among these sheaths the 'intelligent sheath,' having the faculty of knowledge, is an agent. The 'mental sheath,' having the faculty of volition, is an instrument. The 'respiratory sheath,' which has the faculty of action, is a product (of the union of the two former). They say that such is the division of these (three sheaths,) for there is a fitness (in their mutual relations thus regarded). These three sheaths being united form the 'subtile body' (*súkshma Sarira*).[2]

Here also the totality of the subtile bodies, by being the *locus* (seat) of the one intelligence (*sútrátmá*), is collective, like the forest or the lake; and by its being the locus it is more than one intelligence, it is distributive, like the trees or the lake waters.

Intellect *located* in[3] this collective totality (of subtile bodies) is called *sútrátmá* (Thread-soul), because it is passed like a thread through all; it is called *Hiranyagarbha* (Embryo of Light) because it is the superintendent of (that sheath possessing) the power of knowledge; and it is called *Prána* (Life) because it is the superintendent of (that sheath possessing) the power of action.

This collective totality (of the subtile bodies) from its being subtile in comparison with the totality of the gross, is called the subtile body of him (*Hiranyagarbha*). This triad of the sheaths, formed of knowledge, &c., as it is made up of the continuance of our waking thoughts is (called) a dream, and therefore is called the scene of the dissolution of the totality of the gross.[4]

Intellect located in the distributive arrangement of this (aggregate of subtile bodies) is (called) *Taijasa*, (the Resplendent)', because it is located in that inner man which is formed of illumination, (light being the type of knowledge).

This distributive totality (of the subtile bodies) of him (the Resplendent) from its being subtile in comparison with the gross body, is also called the subtile body. It (also) is the triad of sheaths formed of intelligence, &c., and as it is made up of the continuance of our waking thoughts, it is called a dream; and for that reason it (also) is called the scene of the dissolution of the totality of the gross.'

These two, *Sútrátmá* and *Taijasa*, (at the time of one's dreaming) by means of the subtile modifications of the mind, perceive the subtile objects. (This may be inferred) from such texts as "*Taijasa*, the enjoyer of the subtile."[5]

---

[1] "The characteristic of the *rajoguna*." *Jacob.* [2] "It attends the soul in its transmigrations." *Jacob.* [3] "Associated with." *Jacob.*

[4] For then the sight of trees and rivers and the sounds of voices &c., are present to us without the actual things called trees &c., being present at all. To the dreamer the whole external world is as it were not—and, in the opinion of the Vedántin, to the dreamer it really *is* not. Ballantyne. [5] *Mándúkya.* 4.

Here also there is no difference between the collective totality and the distributive totality (of subtile bodies), nor between *Sútrátmá* and *Taijasa*, located therein, just as there is no difference between a forest and its trees, nor between the space occupied by them, and as there is no difference between a lake and its waters, nor between the sky reflected therein.

Thus is the production of the subtile body.

The 'gross elements' (*stúla-bhútáni*) are what have been made (by combining) the five. Making five (is this): Having divided each of the five (elements) Ether, &c., into two equal parts; having next divided severally into four equal parts the five first portions out of those ten portions; the uniting of those four portions,—leaving the (undivided)second half, with the other portions; this is (called) the making (one to possess the various qualities of the) five.[1]

And the doubt is not to be entertained that there is no proof of this, because, by the text which speaks of the combination by threes,[2] the combination by fives is *indicated*. Although the five are alike in respect that each is made up of all the five, yet the name of Ether is appropriate to one and of another to another according to the maxim, "But as they differ, the one is called this, and the other is called that".[3] Then in the Ether sound is manifested; in Air, sound and tangibility; in Fire, sound, tangibility and colour; in the Waters, sound, tangibility, colour, and savour; in Earth, sound, tangibility, colour, savour, and odour.

From these gross elements (having the qualities of the five) arise the worlds that are one above the other, *viz., Bhúr, Bhuvar Svar, Mahar, Janas, Tapas,* and *Satya*; and those that are beneath the other; called *Atala, Vitala, Sutala, Rasátala, Talátala, Mahátala* and *Pátála*; also Brahma's egg (this vaulted world) with the four kinds of gross bodies contained in it, and their food and drink.

The *four kinds of bodies* are the viviparous, oviparous, the moisture-engendered (*svedaja*) and the germinating. The *viviparous* are those produced from a womb, as men and the like. The *oviparous* are those produced from eggs, as birds and snakes; the *moisture-engendered* are those produced from moisture, as lice, gnats.'[4] The *germinating* are those which spring up from the earth, as creepers, trees.

---

[1] Thus a measure—say of eight parts—of any of the gross elements is held to consist of four parts of the subtile element which it bears the name of, and one part of each of the other subtile elements. Hence while the subtile elements are the substrata severally of a single quality—as Ether of sound, Water of savour and so on; the gross elements exhibit the qualities blended, Earth, for example, exhibiting all the five qualities that the five senses take cognizance of." Ballantyne.

[2] *Chhándogya Upanishad*, vi. 3. 3. [3] *Vedánta-Sútra*, 2. 4, 22. See Col. Jacob's remarks on Ballantyne's rendering of it in the Notes to his edition of the Sanskrit text (p.179). Dr.Thibaut renders the aphorism thus:—"But on account of their distinctive nature there is a (distinctive) designation of them" The bháshya says, "By 'distinctive nature' we have to understand preponderance."

[4] No animals are produced simply from moisture. Lice & gnat come from eggs.

Here, too, the gross bodies of the four descriptions (viviparous, &c.,) since they may be the object of cognizance as one or many, are (viewable as) either a collection—as a forest or a lake—or a distributive aggregate—as the trees or as the waters.

Intellect located in this collective aggregate is called *Vaisvánara* (the Spirit of Humanity) and *Virát* (Ruler of the various), because it arrogates to itself that it is all mankind, and because it rules over[1] various forms.

This collective aggregate is the gross body, and since it is a modification of food, it is called the 'nutrimentitious sheath' (*annamaya-kosha*) ; and as it is the scene of the experience of the gross, it is called the waking world, (in contradistinction to the world of dreams).

Intellect located in the distributive aggregate is called *Visva* (the Pervader), because, without abandoning the subtile body, it enters into the gross bodies. This distributive aggregate also is the gross body (of the Pervader) and since it is a modification if food, it is called the 'nutrimentitious sheath'; and as it is the scene of the experience of the gross, it is also called 'the awake.'

Visva and *Vaisvánara* take cognizance of sounds, feelings, colours, savours, and odours by means respectively of the five organs (of sense), whereof hearing is the first, which are presided over in their order by the Sky, the Wind, the Sun, the Regent of the Waters, and the Asvins. (Further, they are concerned about) speaking, taking, walking, evacuating, and enjoying, by means respectively of the five organs (of action) whereof the voice is the first, which are presided over in their order by Agni, Indra, Upendra, Yama, and Prajápati. (Lastly, they are concerned about) judging, determining, feeling, self-consciousness, and thinking by means of the four internal faculties, called mind, intellect, egoism, and thinking, which are presided over in their order by the Moon, Brahmá, Siva and Vishnu. As it is said in the Veda "(The first quarter is Vaisvánara), who is in the waking state and has cognition of externals."[2]

Here too, as before, there is no difference between the distributive aggregate and the collective aggregate of the gross, and between Visva and Vaisvánara, located in these, as (there is none) between the forest and its trees, and between the space occupied by these severally, and as there is none between a lake and its waters, and between the sky as reflected in these severally.

Thus does the gross (or material) world arise out of the five elements intermingled.

---

[1] "Appears in". Jacob.

[2] *Máṇḍukya Upanishad*, 3.

VI.

(THE MEANING OF THE SENTENCE, "TRULY ALL THIS IS BRAHMA;" REFUTATION OF CHARVAKA, BAUDDHA, AND OTHER FALLACIES.)

The collective aggregate of these worlds—the gross, the subtile, and the causal—is one great world; just as the collective aggregate of all the included forests constitutes one great forest; or as the collective aggregate of bodies of water is one great mass of water. Intellect located therein from Vaisvánara up to Isvara is one only; just as the space occupied by the forests included in the great forest, and as the sky (is but one) reflected in the (smaller) bodies of water included (in the great body of water.)

Unassociated intellect, not seen to be distinct from the great world and the intellect associated with it, like a heated ball of iron (in which the iron and the heat are not discriminated), is the literal meaning of the sentence, "Truly all this is Brahma"; but when seen as distinct, it is what is indicated by that sentence."[1]

Thus have we exhibited, under its general aspect, the (great error of) investing the Real with the Unreal.[2]

Now this or that person attributes this or that (erroneous) investment to Soul. The varieties (of opinions) shall now be stated.[3]

A very uncultivated man says, "My *son* is my Soul (better-self);" because the Veda declares that "Soul is born as one's son,"[4] and because one sees that one has love for one's son just as for one's self; and because one feels that "If my son be destroyed or be in good case, I myself am destroyed or am in good case."

A Chárváka[5] says that the gross body is the Soul, because the Veda declares, "This same man (by which is meant the Soul) consists of solid food and juices;[6] and because one sees that one escapes from a house on fire—even leaving one's son; and because one is conscious that "*I* am fat," or "*I* am lean" (so that this "I" must be the body.)

Another Chárváka says that the organs (of sense and action) are the Soul; because the Veda declares that "Those vital airs, having approached Prajápati, said (Lord, which of us is the chief? &c.)"[7] and so on; and because in the absence of the organs, there is the absence of the functions of the body, and because one is conscious that "It is *I* that am one-eyed," or "It is *I* that am deaf."

---

[1] Quoted chiefly from Jacob as clearer than the rendering of Ballantyne.

[2] The error is imputing to Brahma the vesture of a phenomenal world, when there is really no such thing.

[3] Particular aspects of this are pointed out. Each man cites Scripture in favour of his own view; offers a reason, and makes an appeal to consciousness. Ballantyne.

[4] Cf. *Satapatha Brahmana*, 14, 9, 4, 26. [5] Chárváka was a philosopher regarded as an atheist or materialist. He is supposed to have lived before the composition of the Ramáyana. The Chárvákas condemned all sacrificial rites, and called the authors of the Vedas fools and knaves. [6] *Tait. Upanishad*, 2. 1. [7] *Chhándogya*, 5. 1. 7.

Another Chárváka says that the vital airs are the Soul; because the Veda declares that "The other inner Soul is that that consists of the vital airs,"[1] and so on; and because in the absence of the vital airs the organs are not capable of their functions; and because one is conscious that "It is *I* that am hungry," or "It is *I* that am thirsty," &c.

Another Chárváka says that the mind is the Soul because the Veda declares that "The other, the inner Soul, consists of mind,"[2] and so on; and because one observes that, when the mind is asleep, the vital airs are absent; and because one is conscious that "It is *I* who opine," or "It is *I* who doubt."

A Bauddha[3] says that understanding is the Soul, because the Veda declares that "the other, the inner Soul, consists of knowledge;"[4] and because, in the absence of an agent, there is no power in the instrument; and because one is conscious that "It is *I* that act," or "it is *I* that experience."

The Prábhákaras[5] and the Tárkikas[5] say that ignorance is the Soul, because there is the text beginning with "The other, the inner Soul, consisting of joy,"[6] and so on; and because we see that the understanding and the rest resolve into unconsciousness (during profound sleep); and because one is aware that "*I* am ignorant" and that "*I* am cognizant."

The Bhátta[7] says that intelligence united with ignorance is the Soul, because the Veda declares that "The Soul consists of knowledge alone, with much happiness,"[8] &c.; and because in profound sleep there are present both light (in the soul) and the absence of light; and because (every) one has the consciousness that, "Myself I do not know."

Another Bauddha says that nihility[9] is the Soul, because the Veda declares that 'This (universe) previously was simply non-existent,[10] &c., and because in profound sleep everything ceases to exist; and because one, on arising from a deep sleep, has a conviction which has for its object the recollection of his own non-existence.—(thus), "During that deep sleep, I was not."

It shall be now explained how these, beginning with "the son" and ending with "nihility" are *not* the Soul.

As for these mere semblances of scriptural evidence, of argument, and of judgment, adduced by the speakers, from the

---

[1] *Tait. Upanishad*, 2. 2. [2] *Ibid.*, 2. 3. [3] The *Bauddhas* were followers of Buddha, and were regarded as atheists. [4] *Ibid.*, 2. 4. [5] The *Prábhákaras* were the followers of Prabhákara, the well-known scholiast of the Púrva Mímánsá; the *Tárkikas* are the followers of the Nyáya. Jacob.

[6] *Tait. Upanishad*, 2. 5.

[7] The *Bháttas* were followers of Kumarila Bhaṭṭa, a famous teacher of the Mímánsá philosophy and opponent of the Buddhists. He lived before Sankaráchárya.

[8] *Mándúkya*, 5.

[9] Nothingness; the void. Ballantyne.

[10] *Chhándogya*, 6. 2. 1.

"very uncultivated man" downwards, since we see that the seeming texts, arguments, and judgments of each one that comes first are rendered nugatory by the seeming texts, arguments, and judgments of each that follows, it is clear that "the son" or any of the others (suggested) is *not* the Soul.

Moreover, (such opinions are incorrect) because, (first) they are at variance with such very forcible texts as this that "The Soul is not mind, it is not an agent, it is mere Thought existent;" (secondly) because whatever is other than thought, beginning with "the son" and ending with "nihility," is no more *eternal* than a water-jar or the lake, seeing that it is only through Thought that it appears at all; and (thirdly) because the wise man's consciousness, that "I am Brahma" is of more force; and also because each of the *seeming* texts, arguments, and judgments is rendered nugatory (by others); (it follows that) each of these, beginning with "the son" and ending with "nihility," is *not* the Soul.

Therefore, the eternal, pure, intelligent, free, self-existent, and self-evident Thought alone, to which each of these (regarded as the Soul) owes that it appears at all, is the Soul. Such is the direct conviction of those who understand the scope of the Veda.

VII.

(MEANING OF "REFUTATION"; THE PHENOMENAL WORLD ONLY THE ILLUSORY EFFECT OF BRAHMA, WHO IS ITS ILLUSORY MATERIAL CAUSE.)

The "*Refutation*"[1] (of the Erroneous Imputation) is the recognition of the reality itself instead of the unreal world, which, originating in ignorance, envelopes the reality; and this is like the recognition of the rope itself instead of the serpent (the erroneous notion of) which enveloped the rope.

[It has been said, "An actual change of form is called *vikára*, whilst a merely apparent change of form is called *vivartta*." This shall now be illustrated.][2]

This scene of fruition, consisting of the four kinds of gross bodies, and the food and drink and other things in the shape of what is adapted to their fruition, and the fourteen worlds beginning with the Earth which sustain these (bodies), and the substrate of (all) this, Brahma's egg, all this is merely the gross elements which are the cause thereof.

Those (mentioned above) along with Sound and the other objects of sense originating in the gross elements and whatever is the product of the subtile body, all this is nothing else than the unmingled elements which are the cause thereof.

---

[1] "Withdrawal." (*Apaváda*) Jacob.

[2] From Jacob. This extract is omitted in some MSS.

These unmingled elements along with the Qualities, beginning with goodness, in the converse order of their origination, all this is nothing else than Intellect immersed in Ignorance which is the cause thereof.

This Ignorance, and Intellect immersed in Ignorance, taking the shape of Isvara, &c., all this is nothing else than Brahma, 'the Fourth,' in the shape of Intellect not immersed (in any qualities) and which is the substratum of all.

VIII.

(Meaning of "That" and "Thou" in the Great Sentence determined by Erroneous Imputation and its Refutation.)

The clearing up of the sense of the words 'That' and 'Thou' (in the sentence 'Thou art That,') is effected by (a right understanding of) these two—Erroneous Imputation and the Refutation thereof.

(To explain) :—(1) the collective aggregate of Ignorance, (2) Intellect immersed in this and distinguished by the possession of omniscience, &c. (Isvara), and (3) that *not* immersed in this (the 'Fourth') these three, when they seem to be *one*, like a red-hot iron ball, are what the word 'That' *literally* means (the collective aggregate of all things), (again) :—the *real* (or the 'indicated' as opposed to the 'literal') meaning of the word 'That' is the absolute Intellect which is the substratum of that (qualified Intellect) which is immersed therein (*i.e.* in Ignorance).

(Further) :—(1) the distributive aggregate of Ignorance, (2) Intellect immersed in this and distinguished by the possession of partial knowledge (*Prájna*) and (3) that *not* immersed in this (the 'Fourth') these three, when they seem to be *one*, like a red hot iron ball, are what the word 'Thou' *literally* means (any individual in the distributive aggregate of all things), (again) ; the *real* meaning of the word 'Thou' is the absolute Intellect, in the shape of joy, the 'Fourth,' which is the substratum of that (qualified Intellect) which is immersed therein (*i.e.* in Ignorance).

IX.

(Explanation of the Great Sentence, "That art Thou"; the three Relations).[1]

Now the sense of the great sentence shall be explained. This great sentence, 'That art Thou', declares to us, through the three relations, what is meant by 'the Indivisible'.

---

[1] The object is to prove that "That" and "Thou" mean the same thing. This is attempted by showing that the only apparent difference between the senses of

The 'three relations' are (1) the reference to one and the same thing of the two words ('That' and 'Thou') (2) the relation of subject and predicate, in which the things stand that these two words (primarily) denote, and (3) the relation of what is 'indicated' (or really meant) and the 'indicator' which is the relation between pure Soul and the (primary) senses of the two terms ('That' and 'Thou').

This has been declared (by an ancient writer) as follows:—"Reference to the same thing, and the relation of subject and predicate, and the relation of 'indicated' and 'indicator,' are the relations between soul and the primary senses (of 'That' and 'Thou').[1]

(a) *Reference to one and the same thing.*

As, in the sentence, 'That is this same Devadatta,'[2] there is between the word 'That'—which denotes the Devadatta of the previous occasion—and the word 'This,' which denotes the Devadatta of the present occasion—the relation that consists in their both referring to one and the same person; so also, in the sentence 'That art Thou,' there is between the word 'That' which denotes the Soul with the attributes of invisibility, &c. and the word 'Thou' which denotes the Soul with the attributes of visibility, &c. the relation that consists in their both referring to one and the same Intelligence.

(b) *Relation as subject and predicate.*

As in that same sentence ('That is this same Devadatta'), there is between the Devadatta of the prior occasion, who is denoted by the word 'That' and the Devadatta of the present occasion, who is denoted by the word 'This' the relation of subject and predicate, which is constituted by the exclusion of their mutual difference (of time); so also in this sentence ('That art Thou') there is between the Soul with the attributes of invisibility, &c. which is denoted by 'That,' and the Soul with the attributes of visibility, the relation of 'subject and predicate,' which is constituted by the exclusion of their mutual difference, (viz., the Ignorance which is no 'Reality.').

(c.) *Relation as indicator and indicated.*[3]

---

the two terms is that which appears to exist between Ignorance in its *collective* aggregate, and Ignorance in its *distributive* aggregate. As it has been ruled that these have no difference—'as there is none between a forest and its trees'—it follows that there is no difference between the term 'That' and 'Thou' in the sentence 'That art Thou.' Ballantyne.

"The false reasoning is thus pointed out by Ballantyne: "It is tacitly assumed that each tree severally is the forest. The trees might fairly say, '*We* are the forest; but no single one can be suffered to say, 'I am the forest,'—much less can they all be suffered to say this each of himself." p. 83. The reasoning is that a part is identical with the whole.

[1] *Naishkarmyasiddhi*, iii. 3.

[2] "That person whom I saw on some former occasion is this same Devadatta whom I now behold." Ballantyne.

[3] The reasoning will hereafter be shown to be fallacious.

As in the same sentence (That is this same Devadatta) when we leave out the distinction of contradictory times, past and present, belonging to the word, 'That' and 'This,' or to what these primarily denote, then these words stand in the relation of 'indicator and indicated' as regards Devadatta, who is not the contradictory of *himself*; so also in this sentence (That art Thou), when we leave out the contradictory properties, 'invisibility, &c.' and 'visibility, &c.' pertaining to the words 'That' and 'Thou' or to what these primarily denote (the invisible Soul and the embodied Soul), then these words stand in the relation of 'indicator and indicated' as regards the (absolute) Intelligence, which is not the contradictory of *itself*.

This is what is called (in Rhetoric) '*bhágalakshaná*' *i.e.* the indication of a portion.[1]

X.

(Erroneous Explanations of the Great Sentence; the true Meaning.)[2]

In the sentence (That art Thou) the literal meaning of the sentence is not coherent, as it is in the expression, 'The lotus is blue.'[3] In that expression, since the blue—the quality denoted by the word 'blue,' and the lotus—the substance denoted by the word 'lotus, excludes such qualities as 'white,' and such substances as 'cloth,' the literal meaning of the sentence is coherent, because no evidence, from any other quarter, opposes our accepting this as the sense of the sentence that the two are united as subject and attribute, or that either one, to which the other is attributed, is *identical* with it.

But in this sentence ('That art Thou' as opposed to 'The lotus is blue') since the Soul '*invisible, &c.,*' denoted by the word 'That,' and the Soul '*visible* &c.,' denoted by the word 'Thou,' exclude *each other mutually*, the literal meaning of the sentence is *not* coherent, because the evidence of the senses, &c. opposes our accepting this as the sense of the sentence that the two (which

---

[1] According to Hindu rhetoricians, the meaning of every word or sentence comes under one of three heads, that is, it is either literal (*váchya*), indicative (*lakshya*), or suggestive (*vyangya*). 'Indication' is thus defined in the *Kávyaprakása* (ii. 9.): 'When the literal meaning is incompatible (with the rest of the sentence), and either from usage or from some motive, another meaning is indicated, in connection with the primary one, that imposed function is called 'Indication.'" Abridged from Col. Jacob. See *Hindu Pantheism*, pp. 92, 93.

[2] The author now proceeds to contend that the meaning of the 'Great Sentence' cannot be accounted for on other principles of interpretation than those that have been just set forth. Ballantyne.

[3] The 'lotus' being the thing that we call 'blue,' and the 'blue' thing what we call 'lotus.' Ballantyne.

mutually exclude each other) are united as subject and attribute, or that either one, to which the other is attributed, is *identical* with it.[1]

But again, their coherence (in 'That art Thou') is not arrived at by our supposing the terms to be 'indicatory with the relinquishment of their own primary meaning', as is the case in the sentence, 'The herdsman dwells on the Ganges.' In the case of this latter sentence, since there is a *complete* incompatibility in the primary meaning of the sentence which indicates that the Ganges and the herdsman stand in the relation of 'location and located', we *do* arrive at a coherent sense by holding that the case is one of indication with the abandonment of the primary meaning (the word Ganges standing for the *bank* thereof) seeing that it (the stream) is quite qualified to indicate the bank adjoining it.

In this sentence (That art Thou) on the other hand, (as distinguished from 'The herdsman on the Ganges') coherence is not to be arrived at by our supposing the terms to be 'indicatory with the relinquishment of their own primary meaning,' because, since there is only a *partial* incompatibility between the things denoted in the sentence ('That art Thou') which asserts the identity of the invisible Soul and of the Soul visible (as embodied), it would *not* be fit, that, abandoning the residue of the meaning, there should be indicated something else (quite different.)

And you must not say, "as the word 'Ganges,' by relinquishing its own primary meaning, indicates that which is the primary meaning of the word 'bank,' so also let the word 'That' or the word 'Thou', by relinquishing its own primary meaning, convey the meaning of the word 'Thou' or of the word 'That,'; and therefore why does 'Indication with the abandonment of primary meaning' not apply here?" (The two cases differ) because, although, in the case of the one expression,—since, from the word *bank's* not being heard, the sense of that word did not offer itself, —it was to be expected that it should be conveyed by indication; still it was *not* to be expected that, where the sense of the two terms 'That' and 'Thou' *had* been apprehended by the hearing of the terms 'That' and 'Thou,' the sense of each should be conveyed over again, indicatorily, by each term reciprocally.

To this sentence (That art Thou) also (the figure of speech called) Indication *without* relinquishment of the primary meaning, does not apply as it does in the expression 'The Red gallops.' In the case of this expression since the primary meaning is incoherent—purporting, as it does, that a *quality*, viz., 'red' *moves*, the application of 'Indication *without* relinquishment of the primary meaning,' may take place, since we may get rid of the incoherency of the sentence by holding that

[1] The author now proceeds to reject another principle of interpretation on which it has been sought to account for the 'Great Sentence'. Ballantyne.

some *substratum* of the quality—for example a (chestnut) *horse*, is indicated *without* the relinquishment of the primary meaning. But in the case of this expression (That art Thou), the application of 'Indication *without* relinquishment of the primary meaning' cannot take place; because, whilst the primary import of the sentence—viz. the oneness of the invisible and of the (embodied) visible Soul—is incoherent, the incoherence cannot be removed by either terms, indicating anything else whatever in connection with its own primary meaning retained.

And you must not say, 'Let the word 'That' or the word 'Thou' by relinquishing the inconsistent portion of its primary meaning, indicate (severally and reciprocally) the thing meant by the word 'Thou' or by the word 'That'; and why then postulate an indicatory power of another description, viz. 'Indication of a portion'? (This you must not say) because it is impossible that one single word should indicate both a *portion* of its own primary meaning and also the sense of another word, and because no one expects that what has been already intimated by a separate word shall be indicatorily intimated over again.

Therefore, as the sentence 'That is this same Devadatta', or what is primarily meant by the terms thereof—since there is a partial inconsistency in the sentence, importing, as it does, the Devadatta of *prior* times and the Devadatta of the *present* time—having abandoned the inconsistent portion, viz. the being one of prior times and the being one of the present time,—indicates merely that portion of Devadatta which involves no inconsistency;—so also the sentence 'That art Thou,' or what is primarily meant by the terms thereof,—since there is a partial inconsistency in the sentence, importing, as it does, the invisible and the (embodied) visible Soul,—having abandoned the inconsistent portion, viz. the being one possessed of invisibility &c. and the being one possessed of visibility, &c.—indicates merely the Indivisible Intellect, which involves no inconsistency.[1]

XI.

(MEANING OF THE SENTENCE 'I AM BRAHMA'; HE WHO UNDERSTANDS THE GREAT SENTENCE REALIZES HIS UNION WITH IT.)

Now we shall explain the import of that expression of consciousness, 'I am Brahma'. When the meaning of the

[1] This view of the matter may be illustrated algebraically. Not being able to admit as an equation the expression 'Devadatta + past time = Devadatta + present time,' we reflect that the conception of *time* is not essential to the conception of Devadatta's nature; and we strike it out of both sides of the expression which then gives 'Devadatta = Devadatta'.—the equality being that of identity. In the same way, not being able to admit as an equation 'Soul + invisibility = Soul + visibility, &c.' we reflect that the visibility &c. are but the modifications of

'Indivisible' has thus been communicated by means of the sentence (That art Thou), after the teacher has in the foregoing manner cleared up the sense of the two terms 'That' and 'Thou'—then does there occur to the competent student a modification of the understanding[1] as moulded in the form of the 'Indivisible' *viz.*, "I am the eternal, pure, knowing, free, true, self-existent, most blessed Brahma,—(one) without a second."

But this modification of the understanding being accompanied by the reflection of Brahma (thus accurately mirrored in the understanding) having taken as its object what was not previously recognised, *viz.*, the supreme Brahma, who differs not from the individual Soul, puts an end to the 'Ignorance' in respect thereof. Then, as a web is burnt when the yarn that was the cause of it is burnt; so too, when 'Ignorance', which is the cause of all productions, is put an end to, since *every one* of its effects is put an end to, then this modification of the understanding, mirroring the form of the 'Indivisible' is put an end to also—it being one (product) among these (various productions which *all have* 'Ignorance' as their cause.)

As the shine of a lamp, having no power to illuminate the shine of the sun, is overpowered thereby; so too the (reflected) Soul, as reflected in that 'modification of the understanding', through its having no power to illuminate that self-luminous Supreme Brahma, who is none other than the individual Soul, being overpowered thereby, leaves nothing *besides* the Supreme Brahma, who is none other than the individual Soul,—just as, on the removal of a mirror, the reflection of a countenance leaves nothing besides the countenance itself, because that 'modification of the understanding,' which is a portion of that ('Ignorance,') in which He was immersed, has been put an end to (by the recognition of the fact that nothing besides Him exists).

And, the matter standing thus, there is no inconsistency between the two texts of scripture, 'By the mind He is to be apprehended,' &c., and 'who is *not* comprehended by the mind,'[2] &c. because, while admitting that He is made an object of the understanding, we laid down a denial that this involved the (usual) consequence.

And (in regard to the point referred to above) it has been

'Ignorance,' which we are told is no 'reality.' Deleting the unessential portion of each side of the expression, we find Soul = Soul,' the equality being have also that of identity." *Ballantyne.* The reasoning will afterwards be shown to be fallacious.'

[1] *Chittavritti.* The understanding is elsewhere called the 'internal organ. (*antahkarana.*) According to the Vedánta, perception of an object, such as a jar, takes place in the following way: When the eye is fixed upon the jar, the internal organ, with the intelligence appropriated to or reflected in it, goes out towards it, and its light dispels the darkness of Ignorance enveloping it, illuminates it, *assumes its shape,* and so cognises it. *Jacob.* The change is called *Chittavritti.*

[2] *Brihad,* 4, 4, 19. *Kena,* i, 5.

declared as follows: 'Whilst it is necessary that the understanding should be available for the destruction of *ignorance* respecting God, it is denied by the authors of the Institutes that the usual result of this applies to Him also."[1] For again, "Since He is self-luminous there is no need of light (to be thrown on Him.)[2]

There is a (great) difference between a 'modification of the understanding,' when moulded on a material object and this (when mirroring the Supreme Intelligence). To explain;—Suppose we have the case, "This (I perceive) is a jar."—Here, having taken as its object the jar, previously unrecognized, the 'modification of the understanding' mirroring the form of the jar, on dispelling the ignorance that previously attached to the object, throws light upon the jar by the light of its own intelligence; just as the shine of a lamp, when it throws itself upon the surrounding jars, &c., in the dark, on dispelling the darkness illuminates them with its own light:—(but this *usual* sequel to the removal of intervening darkness or ignorance does not apply when the object of theunderstanding is the Supreme Intelligence).[3]

XII.

(Means to be employed to realize the Great Sentence).

Until Intellect (or Deity) becomes in this way directly manifest in its own form, since it is necessary to persevere in (1) hearing (*sravana*), (2) pondering (*manana*, (3) contemplation, (*nididhyásana*), and (4) meditation (*samádhi*), these also shall now be explained.

(*a.*) '*Hearing*' implies the determining through the six characters (or conducers to knowledge) the import of the whole of the theological sections of the Vedas, in regard to the 'Real,' besides which there is nought else. These (conducers to knowledge) are (1) the 'beginning and ending with,' (2) 'inculcation,' (3) novelty,' (4) the 'fruit,' (5) 'eulogizing of the subject,' and (6) 'illustration from analogy.'

1. '*The beginning and the ending* (*upakramopasamhárau*) imply that the matter to be declared in any given section is declared both at the beginning and at the end thereof:—as, for instance, in the sixth section of the *Chhándogya Upanishad*, the 'Real, besides which there is nought else'—which is to be explained in that section —is declared at the outset in the terms "One only, without a second," and at the end in the terms "All this consists of That."

---

[1] *Pancadasi*, vii. [2] *Ibid.*

[3] 'The perception, of Brahma differs from that of an ordinary object in that It, being self-luminous, is not revealed by the light of the intelligence reflected in the internal organ, but shines forth as soon as the latter has dispelled the Ignorance, enveloping It." Jacob.

2. '*Inculcation*[1] &c., (*abhyása*) is the declaration again and again therein of that thing which the section (of the Veda) is concerned with declaring :—as, for example, in that same section the 'Real, besides which there is nought else,' is set forth nine times in the shape of the assertion, 'That art Thou.'

3. '*Novelty*' (*apúrvatá*) here means that the Thing which the section is concerned in declaring is not an object of any other proof; as, for example, in that same section, the truth regarding the 'Real, besides which there is nought else' is not the object of any other proof.

4. By the '*Fruit*' (*phala*) we mean the motive which is heard stated in this or that (section of the Veda), for seeking the knowledge respecting Soul that is brought forward in the section, or for persevering therein; as, for example, in that same section, (vi. 14, 2.), we learn that the inducement for acquiring a knowledge of the 'Real, besides which there is nought else,' is that we may attain to (being ourselves) that (Reality); for, "The man that hath a teacher knoweth (the truth); but he must abide until he be released (from the body); then will he attain (to absorption into the one Reality.)"

5. *Eulogizing of the Subject* (*arthaváda*) is the glorifying of what is set forth in this or that section (of the Veda); as for example, in that same section (vi. 1. 3) the glorifying of the 'Real, besides which there is nought else,' in the following terms: "Thou, O disciple, hast asked for that instruction whereby the unheard of becomes heard, the inconceivable becomes conceived, and the unknowable becomes thoroughly known."

6. "*Illustration from analogy*" (*upapatti*) is the exhibition of a reason, heard stated in this or that (section of the Veda), for the establishment of what is set forth in the section :—as, for example, in that same section (vi. 1-4) we hear stated, as illustrations from analogy, such arguments as the following, to show, when establishing what is the 'Real, besides which there is nought else,' that His (supposed) mutations (are mere figures of speech, or) rest on nothing but words: "O gentle one! as by means of a lump of clay everything that is made of the clay is perfectly known to us,—its modifications or various names, resting merely on language, whilst the truth is that there is (nothing else than) the clay."

(*b*). '*Pondering*' is the dwelling with uninterrupted attention on the 'Real, besides which there is nought else,' which he has heard, together with such illustrations as are in accordance with the Vedántic Doctrine.

(*c*). '*Contemplation*' is the homogeneous flow of the understanding mirroring its object, when this object is the 'Real, besides which there is nought else,'—to the exclusion of the notion of body or any thing heterogeneous (to the one Reality).

---

[1] Repetition. Jacob.

(*d.*) '*Meditation*' (*samádhi*) is of two kinds (1) 'recognising such distinctions as that of subject and object' (*savikalpaka*), and (2) 'recognising no such distinctions as that of subject and object' (*nirvikalpaka*).

(1.) 'Meditation recognising such distinctions as that of subject and object,' consists in the continuance of the understanding in that modification in which it mirrors the 'Real, besides which there is nought else,'—without any concern about the sinking of the distinction between the knower, the knowledge, &c. Then the 'Real, without a second,' *does* shine forth even whilst there is the appearance of duality;—just as there is the recognition of the clay, when we perceive such a thing as an elephant formed of clay. Such (meditations) have been attained by (sages) intent (on emancipation),—in terms such as the following:—'*I* am that being, in the shape of vision, like the ether (all-pervading), pre-eminent, immediately manifest, unproduced, one and imperishable, unsoiled, omnipresent, self-existent, without a second, and for ever free. I am the pure (act of) vision unchangeable; I have no fetter, nor am I *set* free (having always *been* so.)[1]

(2.) 'Meditation which recognises no such distinction as that of subject and object' consists in the continuance of the understanding modified so as to mirror the 'Real, besides which there is nought else,' *with* advertence to the sinking of all distinction between the knower, the knowledge, and the known,—in absolute oneness ("so as to be completely identified with it.")[2]

Then the 'Real, besides which there is nought else,' shines forth *alone*, in the absence of the (separate) recognition of the understanding as mirroring the solitary Reality; just as there appears nothing but the water when the salt, which (on solution) took the form of the water for its own, is no longer recognised.

And you must not entertain the doubt whether there be therefore no difference between this and sound sleep; because, whilst the *non-appearance* of the modification is common to both cases, the two cases differ just in this that it is present in the one case (though not perceived), while in the other (in deep sleep) it is not present at all.

XIII.

(The Eight Means subservient to Meditation without Distinction of Subject and Object.)

The practices subservient to this (*nirvikalpaka samádhi*) are:

1. Forbearance (*yama*).
2. Religious Observances (*niyama*).
3. Postures (*ásana*).

---

[1] *Upadesasahasri*, verse 73. [2] Jacob.

4. Suppression of the Breath (*pránáyáma*).
5. Restraint (*pratyáhára*).
6. Attention (*dhárana*).
7. Contemplation (*dhyána*).
8. Meditation (*samádhi*).

1. Acts of 'forbearance' are not killing, not lying, not stealing, chastity, and not accepting gifts.

2. 'Religious Observances' are purification, contentment, penance, study, and persevering meditation on I'śvara.

3. 'Postures' are the various modes of disposing the hands, feet, &c., spoken of as *padmásana* (lotus posture), *Svastikásana*, &c.

4. 'Suppression of the breath' are those methods for checking respiration, spoken of as slow expiration, slow inspiration, and stopping the breath by shutting the mouth and closing both nostrils with the fingers of the right hand.

5. 'Restraint' is the restraining of the senses from their respective objects.

6. 'Attention' is the fixing of the internal organs upon the solitary Reality.

7. 'Contemplation' is the flowing forth of the internal organ upon the solitary Reality, on separate occasions (not uninterruptedly so).

8. 'Meditation,' here spoken of, is only that which recognises such a distinction as that of subject and object.

To the meditation, *with* exclusion of distinction between subject and object, to which the above are subservient, four things may be obstacles: viz.

1. Listlessness. 2. Distraction. 3. Passion. 4. The tasting of Joy.

1. 'Listlessness' *(laya)* is the sleep of the understanding whilst not sustaining (or mirroring) the Indivisible Reality.

2. 'Distraction' *(vikshepa)* is the understanding's mirroring any thing else instead of mirroring the Indivisible Reality.

3. 'Passion' *(kasháya)* consists in the understanding's not mirroring the Indivisible Reality, even in the absence of 'listlessness' and 'distraction,' through its being paralysed by the fancies of desire, &c.

4. 'The tasting of Joy *(rasásvádana)* is the understanding's experience of felicity, whilst recognizing such distinctions as that of subject and object, when it does *not* mirror the Indivisible Reality; or it is the experience of felicity recognised as distinct from the enjoyer at the time of commencing Meditation.

When the understanding, free from this quaternion of obstacles, like a lamp unagitated when unaffected by the wind, remains simply (in the shape of) the really existent indivisible Intellect, then is there said to be "Meditation recognizing no distinction of subject and object."

It has been said: "When listlessness comes on he should awaken the understanding; when distracted, again, he should quiet it; when assailed by passion, he should bring it to understand; when it has attained to quietism, he should not disturb it; he should not let it enjoy happiness; by rightly discerning he ought to become unattached to these (external and unreal objects)";[1] and again "As a lamp, standing where there is no wind,"[2] &c.

XIV.

(Characteristics of the Jivanmukta.)

Now we shall describe him 'who, yet living, is liberated.' He is 'liberated while yet living,' who, intent on Brahma, is freed from all bonds through the removal of Ignorance and its resultant mass of actions, doubts, and errors, &c., on Brahma becoming manifested as He really is—the Indivisible—through the removal of ignorance in regard to Him—this being consequent on the knowledge of Brahma as He is—the Indivisible, the Pure. This may be inferred from such texts as the following: "When He, the First and the Last, has been discerned, then the knot of the heart is severed, all doubts are resolved, and one's acts are annihilated."[3]

Such a one, with his body, which is a vessel of flesh, blood, urine, excrement, &c., and his set of organs—vessels of blindness, torpor, stupidity, &c., and his mind,—a vessel of hunger, thirst, sorrow, bewilderment, &c.—though beholding the actions that he performs in accordance with this or that preceding fancy, and the fruits of past deeds which he experiences without their obstructing his knowledge (of the truth), does not behold them as realities, for to him they have ceased to exist;—just as the man who knows that so and so is a juggler's trick, though looking upon the illusion, does not look upon it as a reality. (This may be inferred) from such texts as the following: "Seeing, yet as not seeing;—hearing, yet as not hearing." And it has been declared that "He, and no other, knoweth Soul, who, in his waking state, sees not,—just as one in profound sleep (sees not); and who, looking on (what seems) more than one, sees it not under the aspect of duality; so too who, while acting, yet (in his inmost conviction) acts not; this is certain."[4]

As he (the *jívanmukta*) previously to the attaining of right knowledge, followed the ordinary appetites and amusements; so he now follows the impulse to good works only, or else he is alike indifferent to good or bad.

As it is said, "If he who rightly understands that there is no duality may act as he chooses, then what difference is there

---

[1] Gaudapádas *Káriká's*, iii. 44, 45. [2] *Bhagavad Gitá*, vi. 19.
[3] *Mundakopanishad*, 2. 2. 8. [4] *Upadesas'asdhasri*, x. 13.

between *dogs* and those who know the truth—in respect of eating what is unclean ?"[1] (And again, by Sankarácárya) " Abandoning[2] also the fact of his being a knower of Brahma, he knows the Self and no one else does."[3]

Thereon freedom from egotism, and other such perfecters of knowledge, and such good qualities as freedom from malice, will attend him like ornaments. And so it has been declared: "To him who has obtained a knowledge of Soul, such qualities as freedom from malice belong without effort, but these are not now employed as *means*."[4] What more need be said ? This one, merely for the sustenance of his body, acquiescing in the experience of these retributive fruits, in the shape of pleasure or pain procured from desire or aversion on our own part or on another's; and being the spirit that enlightens the modifications of the understanding, on the cessation thereof his life dissolving away into the Supreme Deity, who is unmingled beatitude, on the destruction of Ignorance and the *vis inertiæ* of its results abideth Brahma, in absolute simplicity, unvarying felicity, free from every semblance of difference. (This may be learned from such texts as this,) viz. 'His vital spirit does not transmigrate, but is absorbed'[5]; and, 'absolutely liberated he is absolutely liberated.'[6]

Thus is completed the treatise called the *Vedánta-Sára*, composed by the pre-eminent ascetic, the illustrious Sadánanda, the chief of devotees.

---

[1] *Naishkarmyasiddhi* iv. 62.

[2] A corrected rendering by Col. Jacob instead of the following translation by Ballantyne : "(Well the difference consists) in the knowledge of God. So such a one (as knows God, and not the dog who knows nothing of the truth) being liberated is and no one else is the knower of souls."

[3] *Upadesasáhasrí*, xii. 13.

[4] *Naishkarmyasiddhi* iv. 69.

[5] *Brihadaranyaka*, 4. 4. 6.

[6] *Kathopanishad*, 5. 1.

EXAMINATION

OF

VEDANTISM.

INTRODUCTION.

Definition.—VEDANTISM, in the following remarks, is understood to denote the Advaita (non-dual) theory of Sankara, as explained in his commentary on the Vedánta-Sútras, and as expounded in the *Vedánta-Sára,* and the *Vedánta Paribháshá.* There are other sects who claim to be Vedántists. The principal are the *Visishtádvaita* (qualified non-duality) sect of Rámánuja and the Dvaita (dual) sect of Mádhva, or Ananda-tírtha. The Vallabhas form a third sect. Professor Deussen, during his visit to India, sought to ascertain the percentage of followers belonging to each sect. . A Ramanujist, "a zealous adversary of Sankara, estimated that out of a hundred Vedántins, fifteen perhaps adhere to Rámánuja, five to Mádhva, five to Vallabha, and seventy-five to Sankaráchárya."[1]

Colonel Jacob says in the Preface to his translation of the *Vedánta-Sára* :

"If the people of India can be said to have now any system of religion at all, apart from mere caste observances, it is to be found in the Vedánta philosophy, the leading tenets of which are known to some extent in every village. The subject is therefore one of great importance, and the Vedánta-sára is generally acknowledged to be the most satisfactory summary of the modern phases of it." p. i.

The ESSENCE of the Vedánta is that *nothing exists but Brahma ;* " One only without a second."

PRELIMINARY QUESTIONS.—Indian treatises on any subject often begin with four questions:

" (1) What qualifications are required to render one competent to enter upon the study ?—(2) What is the subject-matter ?—(3) What connection is there between the subject-matter and the book itself ?—and (4) What inducement is there to enter upon the study at all ? The answer to each of these questions is called an *anubandha*—a 'bond of connection' or 'cause'—because, unless a man knows what a book is about, and whether he is competent to understand it, and what good the knowledge will do him, he cannot be expected to apply himself to the study of the book, instead of employing himself otherwise."[2]

The above points and others arising out of them are considered in the Second Section into which the Vedánta-Sára has been divided.

---

[1] Address at Bombay, 25th February, 1893.

[2] *The Pandit* for July, 1867, p. 46. Quoted by Colonel Jacob.

"The Competent Person."—The Vedánta-Sára begins by describing the *adhikárin*, the person qualified to undertake the study. The qualifications are thus summarised by Dr. Mullens:

"He must first find out the sense of the Vedas, as books of the language, by the study, according to rule, of the Vedángas. He must either in his present birth, or in a preceding one, renounce all the objects of desire, such as sacrifices which obtain heaven, and works which are forbidden, as Brahman murder and the like. By the performance of the *Sandhyá bandhana*, and other appointed ceremonies; by offering expiations; and engaging in acts of internal worship, he must purify his mind from errors, and fix it upon Brahma."[1]

"The Four Requisites."—Here also the summary of Mullens may be given:—

(1.) He must distinguish between the *real* and *unreal*; *i.e.*, he must regard everything unreal except Brahma. (2.) He must free himself from all *desire* of enjoying the fruits of merit, whether in this life or a future one. (3.) He must exclude from his mind and from sense everything which does not refer to Brahma. He must endure cold and heat, pleasure and pain, without recognizing a difference between them. (4.) He must have an intense desire after *liberation* from self, and absorption into Brahma. These exercises duly completed, he will be qualified to learn more. With earnestness of soul, let him now hasten to a teacher, with offerings in his hand, and becoming his disciple, beg him to impart that knowledge which is the highest that can be attained."[2]

The Subject.—This is that the Soul and Brahma are one—the drift of all Vedánta treatises.

The End.—The removal of the ignorance regarding the identity of Soul and Brahma—and the attainment of the joy which is the essence of Brahma. "Thus aided," says Mullens, "by divine choice; thus prepared by ritual services, by self-subjugation, and by the desire of obtaining the knowledge of the Supreme; and thus provided with a competent teacher, the student must place himself at his master's feet, to receive with undoubting faith whatever that master may choose to teach."

To enable the reader to form his own judgment of Vedántism, a summary has been given of the Vedánta-Sútras, and the Vedánta-Sára has been quoted in full. Some remarks will now be offered on its leading tenets from the standpoint of the Nineteenth Century.

While the subjects discussed in the Vedánta-Sára will be considered, its arrangement will not be followed. The chief dogma will first be examined, and then others with which it is connected.

---

[1] *Hindu Philosophy*, p. 119. [2] *Ibid*, p. 120.

THE CHIEF DOCTRINE OF ADVAITISM.

This is briefly stated in two celebrated formulas:

Ekam evádvitíyam, "ONE ONLY WITHOUT A SECOND."
Sarvam Khalvidam Brahma, "ALL THIS (UNIVERSE) IS BRAHMA."

Rammohun Roy and Keshub Chunder Sen interpreted the first to signify that there is only one God; but the real meaning is that nothing exists but God—a very different doctrine. The second formula expresses it clearly. It declares that all that exists is Brahma.

THE FOUNDATION OF ADVAITISM.

In the twilight a rope is mistaken for a serpent.
Mother-of-pearl is mistaken for silver.
A thousand suns may be seen in a thousand pots of water.

Conclusions.

The universe, supposed to be real, is only imaginary, like the serpent or mother-of-pearl.

Our souls are only like the reflection of the sun in the pots of water: Brahma is the only real existence.

On this very slender basis the lofty superstructure of Advaitism has been reared.

Grand Defect of Hindu Reasoning.—This is to *accept illustration as argument.* That there may be several roads to the same city is regarded as proving that all religions lead to God. Ramakrishna, the guru of Swami Vivekananda, expressed it thus:

"As one may ascend to the top of a house by means of a ladder or a bamboo or a staircase or a rope, so divers are the ways and means to approach God, and every religion in the world shows one of these ways."

Ramakrishna's argument amounts to this: "As there are several ways of getting to the top of a house, so atheism and polytheism, pantheism and monotheism are all true." Swami Vivekananda, with logic equal to that of his Guru, said at Chicago, "We accept all religions to be true."

One illustration may appear to prove one thing, but another may be adduced leading to an opposite conclusion. It is sometimes said, "As there is only one sun in the sky, so there is only one God." This is a great truth, but the reasoning is no better than the following, "As there are innumerable stars in the sky, so the number of gods is countless."

Kapila justly says: "**There is no acceptance of the inconsistent, else we come to the level of children, madmen, and the like.**"[1]

[1] *Sánkhya Aphorisms*, Book I.

Advaitism is based on "ILLUSORY ANALOGIES OF DEDUCTIONS FROM FALSE PREMISES."

Before considering at length the formula, "One only without a Second," some account will be given of *Avidyá* and *Máyá*, invented to explain away the apparent reality of the Universe.

AVIDYA AND MAYA.

When a man makes one false statement, he is often obliged to invent others for its support. Advaitists, starting with the false assumption that nothing exists but Brahma, are forced to devise another to account for what is so opposite to the evidence of our senses. The result is the figment of *Avidyá* and *Máyá*.

Avidya.—*Vidyá* means knowledge; *avidyá* means non-knowledge or Ignorance. Thibaut explains "*adhyása* as literally 'superimposition,' in the sense of (mistaken) ascription or imputation to something of an essential nature or attributes not belonging to it." "The Vedánta-Sára says that "Erroneous Imputation" or "Illusory Attribution" is supposing the unreal to be real; as when a rope is imagined to be a serpent.

Avidyá is said to be neither existent nor non-existent. Ballantyne thus describes its two *powers*:

> "Ignorance has two powers; that by which it *envelopes* soul, giving rise to the conceit of personality or conscious individuality, and that by which it *projects* the phantasmagoria of a world which the individual regards as external to himself."[1]

Sankara thus explains *avidyá*:

> "This superimposition, thus defined, learned men consider to be *Avidyá*, and the ascertainment of the true nature of that which is (the Self) by means of the discrimination of that (which is superimposed on the Self) they call Knowledge (*Vidyá*).")[2]

The explanation of Sankara is not very lucid. The following seems to be the main point: So long as a man imagines himself to be different from Brahma, he is in a state of *Avidyá*. When he can say *Brahmásmi*, 'I am Brahma,' then he possesses *Vidyá*, and is the wise man.

Maya.—The meaning of *Máyá* has varied. The *Brahmavádin* thus describes the changes:

> "A reference to the *Sarvánukramaniká* of Kátyáyana shows us that the word Máyá occurs in many of the hymns of the Rig-Veda, in almost all its different grammatical forms, and is used in connection with several of the gods whose praises are sung therein. In all these places Sáyana invariably interprets *Máyá* to mean *prájná* (intelligence). In Yáska's

---

[1] *Christianity contrasted with Hindu Philosophy*. p. xxxvi.

[2] *Vedánta-Sútras*, Vol. I. p. 6.

Nirukta it is derived from *má*, to measure; and is made to mean thereby the intelligence through which all things are measured and comprehended. There are also a few places where Máyá is interpreted as 'wonderful power.'

"The Vedánta is based on the Upanishads: but in these scriptural discourses on philosophy and religion there is no system; and it has been the endeavour of the *Sútrakára*, the composer of the aphorisms and his commentators, to evolve a system out of the materials furnished by them. The word Máyá scarcely occurs in the principal Upanishads. But where it does occur it seems to be used mostly in the old Vedic sense. The only two Upanishads where this word may be taken to be used in a new sense are the *Svetásvatara* and *Maitráyani*. However it is quite certain that the philosophic system of thought which subsequently grew out of the Upanishads led to the elaboration of the Vedántic idea of Máyá . . .

"The import of Máyá as matured by Sankara in his Advaita system is partly an internal growth of the Upanishads and partly due to the Máyá theory of the Buddhists against whom Sankara mainly contended."[1]

In the Vedas the reality of the external world is recognised. In the Upanishads generally Brahmá is the *material* cause of the world as well as its *efficient* cause. He is compared to a spider, weaving its web out of its own body. This will be noticed more fully under "Creation." The supposed illusory nature of external objects was a later development.

Dr. Krishna Mohun Banerjea attributes the origin of Máyá to Buddhism:

"Vyasa does not inculcate that doctrine, nor do the Upanishads, Taittiriya, *Aitareya*, and *Kena*. Vijnána Bhikshu, in his commentary on the Sánkhya Sútra (i. 22), draws a marked distinction between the Brahma Sútras and the theory of Máyá. 'There is not a single Brahma Sútra,' says he, in which our bondage is declared to be a mere deception. As to the novel theory of Máyá, propounded by persons calling themselves Vedántists, it is only a species of the Vijnána-váda (of Buddhists). The commentator then quotes the well-known passage in the Padma-Purána in which that theory is called *disguised Buddhism*. He proceeds to say, 'that theory is not a tenet of the Vedánta, and it must be understood that the doctrine of the new fangled disguised Buddhists, who assert the theory of Máyá and reduce our bondage to a mere delusion is in this way refuted.'"[2]

"It is only in the *Svetásvatara* that we have the theory of Máyá, and we hear of God as its projector in the sense of a juggler."[3]

Máyá now generally means 'illusion' or 'power of illusion.' Gough says:

"The world, with its apparent duality of subject and object, of external and internal orders, is the figment of Máyá, the imagination of illusion. . . . All the stir of daily life, all the feverish pleasures and pains of

[1] *Brahmavádin*, Vol. I. pp. 295, 296.
[2] *Dialogues on Hindu Philosophy*, p. 313. [3] *Ibid*, p. 321.

life, after life, are the phantasmagory of a waking dream. For the soul that wakes to its own nature these things cease to be, and, what is more, have never so much as been."[1]

Avidyá and *Máyá* are often used as synonymous: but, strictly, *Avidyá* is the *cause* and *Máyá* the *effect*.

THREE MODES OF EXISTENCE.

The gradual development of the doctrine of *Máyá* has been described. The *Paribháshá* gives a later refinement, unknown to Sankara—that of the *three modes of existence*. These are defined as *páramárthika*, real, *vyávahárika*, practical, and *prátibhásika*, apparent. Brahma is the only *real* existence. I'śvara, individual souls, heaven, hell, the earth and all that it contains, are said to be imagined by ignorance, and to have no more true existence than things seen in a dream. Only the ignorant mistake them as existent, and by means of them transact *practical* life; whence the epithet. The *apparent* include such things as a rope imagined to be a snake, nacre mistaken for silver, &c.

The three modes of existence were invented by Vedántins to support the doctrine of non-duality. Dr. K. Mohun Banerjea says:

"The denial of a world, which was evident to all our senses, was itself so much opposed to nature and common sense, that they taxed their ingenuity as far as they could, to qualify that denial. They introduced the terms *Vyávahárika* and *páramárthika*, or *conventional* (or practical) and *real* existences, in order to save their doctrine. The former they attributed, the latter they denied, to the world. If asked, *how all this can be God*,—they would tell you the material world was a *Máyá*, an illusion."

"If however charged, on the other hand, with the absurdities, so well set forth in the *Vidwanmodatarangini*, they instantly shift from their position, and tell you they did not entirely deny the visible world. It had an existence in *vyavahára*, though it was *paramárthatah*, no reality.

"But the soul of man itself has no other than *vyávahárika* existence. Do you think you are an entity?—You may be one in popular parlance—you are not so *paramárthatah*, in reality. 'This one,' says the Vedánta-Sára, 'which fancies itself to be agent and patient, and passes to and fro between this and the other world, is called the *vyaváhárika jíva*, or conventional soul.'"[2]

Dr. K. Mohun Banerjea thus denies the doctrines of three modes of existence:

"Now there can be no such thing as a substance existing *conventionally*, but not *really*. Things there may be existing in the opinions of man, or implied in their conduct, but if we deny their reality, we can only mean that they are mere fancies, and therefore not actually existing

[1] *Philosophy of the Upanishads*, p. 48. [2] *Dialogues on Hindu Philosophy*, p. 391.

substances. Sankaráchárya has said what it is impossible to gainsay, 'that the question of the reality of a substance is not dependent on human notions. It depends on the substance itself. To say of a post that it is either a post, or a man, or something else, is not to enunciate the truth. That it is a man or something else is a false notion. That it is a post is alone the truth, since it is dependent on the substance itself ' Thus the determination of an existing substance depends ' on the substance itself.' It must either exist, or not exist, whatever men may say or think. In fact conventional, as opposed to real, can only mean imaginary, in other words, false."[1]

Parinamavadins and Vivartavadins.—*Parináma* denotes change, modification; *vivarta* denotes illusory manifestation of Brahma. The *Parinámavádins* hold that the world is the effect of Brahma's undergoing a real change; while the latter maintain that it is only illusory. The former is undoubtedly the older view. In the Vedánta-Sútras, Brahma is held to be the material cause of the universe.

Avidya eternally associated with Brahma.—Gough says:

" Brahman *per se* is the principle of reality, the one and only being; Self alone is, and all else only seems to be. This principle of unreality, however, has been from everlasting associated with an inexplicable principle of unreality; and it is from the fictitious union of these principles, the one real, the other only a self-feigned fiction, that the spheres and the migrating forms of life, the external and internal world, proceed."[2]

Avidya admitted to be inexplicable.—Deussen says:

" All the different actions in the world and the various forces developed thereon, all depend on Ignorance (*Avidyá*) or false knowledge. All enquiry rebounds from this idea of *Avidyá*. Whence this ignorance arises which is innate in us, we do not learn."[3]

Max Müller says:—

" To know what this Nescience or *Avidyá* is, is impossible, nay self-contradictory."[4]

But absurdity does not trouble a Hindu. Purushottama Misra says: " In this system which maintains that everything transcends explanation, unreasonableness is no objection."

Avidya, a mere assumption.—The *Vedántasiddhántamuktávalí*, as translated by Professor Venis, says[5]:

" Of the reality of Avidyá there is no evidence, revealed or human. . . . Is Avidyá proved by Veda or by perception, &c., or is it assumed to account for the world of experience, which cannot otherwise be accounted for? Not by Veda, nor by perception, inference, or human teaching; For, if by any of these *Avidyá* were clearly proved, controversy would be at an end. And since there is no evidence for *Avidyá*, it must need

---

[1] *Dialogues*, pp. 394, 395. [2] *Philosophy of the Upanishads*, pp. 45, 46.
[3] *Short Account of the Vedánta Philosophy*, p. 13.
[4] *Vedánta Philosophy*, p. 99. [5] Quoted by Col. Jacob.

be granted that *Avidyá* is *assumed* to account for the otherwise inexplicable production of the unreal world . . . . For there is no other course apart from this assumption of *Avidyá.*" pp 14, 15.

Maya charges God with Deception.—Deussen says:

"The whole world is illusion (*máyá*) which Brahman, as a magician (*máyávin*), draws out of himself, and by which as magician he is in no way affected; or by another turn of the picture Brahman becomes through Ignorance (*avidyá*), as the magician by his magic, indistinctly seen. He is the cause of the world as the magician of his magic, the cause of the withdrawal of the world into his own self, like as the earth draws into itself all living beings." [1]

The whole universe is a gigantic lie, and the Liar is the Supreme Brahma!

To the above Dr. K. Mohun Banerjea replies:

"You say the world is a *máyá*, an illusion, and that God is the *máyí*, the conjurer who thus deceives you. Is it not grossly revolting to our moral feelings to say that God has deliberately projected a false appearance with a view to beguile rational minds of His own creation?

"We are all agreed that religious errors are the most serious of all errors, and of all religious errors the greatest must be that which consists in a false notion of Divine Attributes. Is it possible to believe that God would deliberately produce such an error in His creatures?" [2]

How can Maya be known?—The question has been asked:

"If my consciousness is deceived by Máyá, how am I to know it? My very knowledge itself is illusion; all things within me and around me are products of illusion, deception, and error. How then am I to know them to be such? The knowledge of the illusion is itself an illusion, and the power which recognises the confusion is itself confused. Hence the knowing mind denies the illusion altogether, and the effort to deny it proves it is untrue." [3]

Contradictory Assertions about Ignorance.—Nehemiah Goreh has the following remarks on this point:

"Vedántins say that the world does not really exist, but appears to exist through Ignorance. But does that Ignorance really exist? Surely it must really exist, for if it did not really exist what would cause the false world to appear true? But they cannot admit that Ignorance really exists, for if they admit Ignorance to be an entity additional to Brahma, their doctrine of non-duality will, as Párthasárathi says, perish. Moreover, if Ignorance be real, Brahma itself must be believed to be its subject, but that would again contradict their doctrine that Brahma is ever free from Ignorance; they say therefore that Ignorance also is not real. It does not really exist, but, like the world, is imagined to exist, and therefore false. But by whom as it imagined to exist? By itself is the reply. Is not absurdity now carried to the highest pitch? But is it

---

[1] *Short Account of Vedánta Philosophy*, p. 13, Madras Ed.

[2] *Dialogues*, pp. 398 and 406, 407. [3] *Vedántism, &c.*, by Mullens, p. 149.

possible for the human mind to believe that a thing which does not exist can imagine itself to exist? Though then they call Ignorance false, they feel in their hearts that it really exists. All their talk about various kinds of existence is mere nonsense. There is only one kind of existence."[1]

Realities.—Mr. Slater well says:

"The God who made us, made us *real*; and real we must remain for all eternity. God is real, the world is real, self is real, sin is real, and judgment real enough to make men tremble. There is no *Máyá* but what man cheats himself to imagine. Some day the awful reality of everything will be brought home to us in such force that escape will be impossible. To grasp reality now is the only way to avoid being grasped by it hereafter."[2]

The question of Máya is also discussed under the next head.

"ONE ONLY WITHOUT A SECOND."

This leading doctrine of Vedántism will now be considered.

1. **It is a dogma unsupported by proof—a mere assumption.**—As already mentioned, its only basis is that in the twilight a rope may be mistaken for a serpent, mother-of-pearl for silver.

2. **It is contradicted by the evidence of all our senses under the most favourable circumstances for forming a correct judgment.**—Kanáda has well said that it is only when the senses are unsound or defective, or when some bad habit is contracted that a person may be deceived. Even if one sense is deceived, the other senses disabuse the mind. The rope can easily be found by the touch not to be a serpent. All our senses at noonday, when we are in the enjoyment of perfect health, testify to the real existence of the external world.

Sankara himself, when arguing with Buddhists, admitted the evidence of the senses:

"To all this we reply that external things do exist. It is impossible to judge that external things have no existence; and why? because we are conscious of them. In every act of perception some or other outward thing is presented to the consciousness, be it post or wall, or cloth or jar, or whatever else it may be; and that of which we are conscious cannot but exist. If a man, at the very moment he is conscious of outward things through his senses, tells us that he is not conscious of them, and that they have no existence, why should we listen to him, any more than we should listen to a man who in the moment of eating and enjoying told us that he was not eating and was not enjoying what he ate?"[3]

Nehemiah Goreh argues similarly:

"I demand of the Vedántins, How is that you assert falseness of the world, which is certified to us, by senses, &c., to be true? Since

---

1 *Indian Church Quarterly Review*, April 1891, pp. 148, 149.
2 *Studies in the Upanishads*, p. 56.
3 Quoted by Gough. *Philosophy of the Upanishads*, pp. 192, 193.

you thus despise those proofs, what credit can be attached to anything that you advance? Proceeding in this way, you unsettle the foundations of everything, whether as regards this world, or as regards the next. And on your own grounds, how can you refute the doctrines of others, or establish your own?

"Perhaps you will urge, that, since the senses, &c. often deceive us, they are totally unreliable. For instance, we are sure, that we see chariots, elephants, and other things, in our dreams; and yet they are proved to be false. I reply, that, if a seeming proof is made out, by a real proof, to be faulty, we reject it. But how can we contemn a proof which cannot be shown to be faulty? As for the things that we see in dreams, we call them false, because, on awaking, we find them to be so; and their falsity, as being matter of every-day experience, is indubitable. But who has ever found the external objects of nature to be false? Has not every man of all generations borne evidence to their truth?

"If you say, that, to a man in dreamless sleep, the world disappears, and that his experience goes to disapprove the truth of the world, I demur to the conclusion; since, a man's cognition being then suspended, he cannot be brought forward as witness for anything that then had place. It is the belief of the Vedántins, that, even in dreamless sleep, there subsists a sort of cognition. Let this be granted: still, external things are not proved, thereby, to be false. To form any jdgment whatever about them is not competent to this cognition; and therefore, it cannot conclude their falsity. In like manner, a blind man is able to appreciate sound, touch, &c., but not colours; and so he can be no witness of their truth, or of their falseness."[1]

3. **It is refuted by our Natural Convictions.**—"An English philosopher says that while man has the exclusive privilege of forming general theorems, he has also a monopoly of the *privilege of absurdity;* to which no other living creature is subject. *And of men,*" he adds, "those *are of all most subject to it that profess philosophy.*" Cicero had the same opinion. "There is nothing so absurd," says he, "which has not been held by some philosopher." To none does this apply more than to Hindu philosophers. As Monier Williams remarks, "The more evidently physical and metaphysical speculations are opposed to common sense, the more favour do they find with some Hindu thinkers."[2] Mr. Slater says,

> "A system, however logical, condemns itself, when it contradicts any of those natural convictions which are intended, as Dr. Thomas Brown says, to save us from the folly of our own ratiocinations."[3]

The Latin for 'I' is *ego,* and *non* means 'not.' We naturally distinguish between the *ego,* and the *non-ego,* the 'I' and the 'not I,' the subject and the object, ourselves and things around us. No one but a learned fool need ask, like Ribhu in the Vishnu

---

1 *Rational Refutation,* pp. 170, 171.
2 *Brahmanism and Hinduism,* p. 87.
3 *Studies in the Upanishads,* pp. 47-50.

Purana (II. 16), "which is *you* and which is *I?*" The doctrine of non-duality is therefore refuted by our natural convictions.

4. **It is contradicted by Reason.**—This is shown in different ways. Flint says:

"Vedántism admits that besides the one real being there are appearances or illusions. But even appearances or illusions are phenomena which require to be explained. And they cannot be explained on the hypothesis of absolute unity. They imply that besides the absolute being there are minds which can be haunted by appearances, which can be deluded into believing that these appearances are realities."[1]

The universe contains countless objects differing widely from each other—mineral, vegetable, and animal. Among the last some are constantly engaged in devouring one another. With what reason can it be alleged that only one being exists?

Lastly, it leads to the blasphemous assertion, Brahmásmi, 'I am Brahma.' This will be noticed at length under another head.

5. **Vedantism cuts at the roots of Morality.**—A writer in *Awakened India* makes an opposite claim:

"The Vedánta philosophy shows that the relation between man and God is far closer and more intimate than that set forth by any other system. It establishes the identity of the human soul with the Supreme Soul, and thus inculcates a higher morality." Sept. 1897.

If the human soul and the Supreme Soul are identical, then the latter is responsible for every action of the former. As He is the sole being, every action that is performed is an action of God. The most wicked deeds which men vainly fancying themselves free agents are tempted to perform, are actually perpetrated by God. Flint says:

"The worst passions and vilest actions of humanity are states and operations of the One Absolute Being. Man cannot be justly held responsible for what truly belongs to God—for affections or deeds which are necessarily manifestations of the Divine nature."[2]

According to Vedantism, "The distinctions of right and wrong are mere appearances which will vanish as soon as the dream state of life is dispelled." The *Brahmavádin* says:

"If we know that there is nothing else but the A'tman, that everything else is but a dream, that the world's poverties, its miseries, its wickedness and goodness are mere delusions and hallucinations, then we become Jnána Yogins." June 5, 1897.

"Wickedness and goodness mere delusions and hallucinations!" Prahláda says to Vishnu, "Thou art knowledge and ignorance, thou art truth and falsehood; thou art poison and

---

1 *Anti-Theistic Theories*, pp. 418, 419. 2 *Anti-Theistic Theories*, p. 395.

nectar."[1] The eternal distinction between right and wrong is thus blotted out.

According to Swami Vivekananda, Vedántism says: "Our evil is of no more value than our good, and our good of no more value than our evil."[2]

Man feels himself a free agent and responsible for his conduct. Conscience is the highest principle of the human spirit. Vedántism contradicts its most sacred and certain convictions, and directly tends to deaden and destroy it.

Flint says:

> "Right and wrong are absolutely exclusive of each other. There can be no compromise between them, or reconciliation of them. They cannot blend and merge into any common higher result. The one can only be satisfied by the annihilation of the other. All this pantheism is logically necessitated to deny, but in so doing dashes itself against a rock."[3]

It has been shown that the dogma of non-duality, "One only without a second," is

1. A mere Assumption, unsupported by proof.
2. That it is contradicted by the Evidence of all our Senses, under the most favourable circumstances for forming a correct judgment.
3. That it is refuted by our Natural Convictions.
4. That it is contradicted by Reason.
5. That it cuts at the roots of Morality, making God the author of every crime perpetrated.

For the reasons given, it is evident that the Advaita theory is a mere fiction, invented by a few so-called philosophers. The great bulk of mankind, including the wisest and best that have ever lived, have always held the distinction between the Creator and His creatures. As Tennyson says:

> "Eternal form shall still divide
> The eternal Soul from all beside."

Some other Vedantic doctrines will next be examined.

BRAHMAN OR BRAHMA.

"As is the god so is the worshipper."[4]—There is no more important question for a nation than this, What is the nature of the God it worships?

> "The worshipper looks upon the character of the object which he worships as the standard of perfection. He therefore condemns everything in himself which is unlike, and approves of everything which is like that character. The tendency of this is to lead him to abandon everything

---

1 *Vishnu Purána*, I. 19.
2 *Brahmavádin*, Jan. 19th, 1897.
3 *Anti-Theistic Theories*, p. 403.
4 *Yathá devah, tathá bhaktah.*

in himself and in his course of life, which is condemned by the character and precepts of his god, and to conform himself to that standard, which is approved by the same criterion. The worshipper desires the favour of the object worshipped, and this, reason dictates, can be obtained only by conformity to the will and the character of that object. To become assimilated to the image of the object worshipped must be the end of desire with the worshipper. His aspirations, therefore, every time he worships, do, from the nature of the case, assimilate his character more and more to the model of the object that receives his homage.

"To this fact the whole history of the world bears testimony. Without an exception, the character of every nation and tribe of the human family has been formed and modified in a great degree, by the character attributed to their gods."[1]

"Show me your gods," said an old Greek writer, "and I will show you your men." Long ago Aristotle remarked: "Men create the gods after their own image, not only with regard to their form, but also with regard to their manner of life." Cicero said of his countrymen and the Greeks, "Instead of the transfer to man of that which is Divine, they transferred human sins to their gods and experienced again the necessary action."

The gods of the Hindus are typical of themselves at different periods in their history. In Vedic times Indra is the soma-drinking martial god who recovers the celestial cows from the fort of Pani, and helps the Aryans in their wars against the aborigines. When the Aryans had overcome their enemies and were settled in India, Indra, as described in the Puranas, "is a gorgeous king of a luxurious and somewhat voluptuous court, where dance and music occupy most of his time." The gods of the Puranas are Hindu Rajas, with their tastes and surroundings, but possessed of superhuman powers.

After the dogma of transmigration was accepted and a pessimistic view was taken of life, a new type of God was invented, called Brahma. It was supposed to exist in a state of dreamless sleep, happy in being free from the miseries of *samsára*. It was called "Brahman (nominative neuter, Brahmă, from the root *brih*, 'to expand,' because it expanded itself through all space. It was a pure essence which not only diffused itself everywhere, but constituted everything. Men, gods, the visible world were merely its manifestations."[2]

It is very important to discriminate between Brahman or Brahma, neuter, from Brahmá, masculine, denoting Brahma with attributes. To avoid confusion the latter will be called *I'svara*, the Lord. The former is also called Parama A'tman, the highest spirit or self.

---

[1] *Philosophy of the Plan of Salvation.* See also Psalm cxxxv. 18.
[2] Monier Williams, *Brahmanism and Hinduism*, p. 21.

Attributes of Brahma.

The general confession is made that Brahma is *unknowable.*[1] *The Brahmavádin* says:

"The fundamental doctrine of agnosticism, 'that God is inaccessible to human thoughts and words', is also accepted by the Vedánta, and is in entire accord with the general view of its theology.' Reason can describe the Lord only as '*na iti,' na iti,*' as 'No','No.'" Vol. II. p. 65.

While making this acknowledgment of nescience, the Vedántists have not scrupled to dogmatise about Brahma as if they were fully acquainted with its nature. Some of their assertions will now be noticed.

Brahma Impersonal.—The question might first be asked, If Brahma is unknowable, how can it be affirmed that It is impersonal? The chief idea is that Brahma is not conscious of Its own existence. Hindu philosophers generally think this a higher state than the opposite. Deussen says that we should not "think so low of God as to impute him personality."[2]

As the question is of great importance, it will be considered at some length. There is a whole volume on the subject by Illingworth, *Personality Human and Divine,* from which a few extracts will be taken.

Meaning of Personality.—Person usually denotes a bodily form; but this is not the sense in which it is here understood. Illingworth says:

"The fundamental characteristic of personality is self-consciousness, the quality in a subject of becoming an object to itself, or in Locke's language, 'considering itself as itself,' and saying 'I am I.'"[3]

A consciousness of our own existence, in Tennyson's words, "power to feel 'I am I'"[4] is the first point. It is evident that a pure spirit may have this feeling as well as one connected with a material body.

But more is included. Secondly, Illingworth says:

"Our self-consciousness involves freedom, or the power of self-determination....The freedom of the will does not mean the ability to act without a motive...but it does mean the ability to create or co-operate in creating our own motives, or to choose our motive, or to form a weaker motive into a stronger by adding weights to the scale of our own accord, and thus to determine our conduct by our reason; whence it is now usually called the power of self-determination."[5]

---

[1] There is a valuable work by Iverach, *Is God Knowable?* 3s. 6d. Hodder and Stoughton.

[2] *Short Account of Vedánta Philosophy,* p. 13.

[3] *Personality, Human and Divine,* p. 28.

[4] *Higher Pantheism.* [5] *Personality,* &c. p 3.

Thirdly, Illingworth says, "Desire is a co-essential element in our personality."

"These, then, are the constituent elements of personality, as such—self-consciousness, the power of self-determination, and desires which irresistibly impel us into communion with other persons—or, in other words, reason, will, and love. These are three perfectly distinct and distinguishable functions, but they are united as being the functions of one and the selfsame subject." p. 38.

Impersonality implies the absence of self-consciousness, self-determination, and desire. The Impersonal Brahma is unconscious of Its own existence; It neither determines nor desires. Its condition is fitly represented by dreamless sleep. The Vedánta-Sútras (I. iii., 42) say, "And (on account of the designation) (of the highest Self) as different (from the individual soul) in the states of deep sleep and departing." Sankara, in his Commentary, says, "We thus understand that 'on account of his being designated as something different in the states of deep sleep and departure,' the highest Lord forms the subject of the passage."[1] A person in a dreamless sleep is not self-conscious, he has no self-determination, he is desireless. The more nearly a person resembles this, the more he is like Brahma. The following explanation is abridged from Ballantyne:

"A person wide awake in the full possession of all his faculties is considered as being furthest removed from Brahma, being enveloped in the densest investment of *Avidyá*. This is said to be the first quarter. During dreamy sleep, he is considered to have shuffled off the outermost coil, and so far resembles Brahma. This is called the second quarter. Dreamless sleep is the third quarter. The *átman* is then supposed to be united with Brahma. For the time being the *átman* is now 'pre-eminent in being as no longer exposed to the varied miseries that arise from the fictitious semblances of duality.' On awaking it returns to the first quarter."

The Vedánta-Sútras thus explain what takes place in a swoon:

"In him who is senseless (in a swoon, &c.,) there is half-union; on account of this remaining (as the only possible hypothesis)."

Sankara, after a long commentary, comes to the conclusion "Therefore those who know Brahman declare a swoon and the like to be a half-union."[2]

In the scale of creation, a plant is higher than a stone, a beast than a plant, a man than a beast. Is it consistent with common sense to suppose that a man in dreamless sleep, unconscious of his own existence, stands on a higher level than the same person cognizant of all around him and able to benefit his fellow-creatures?

---

[1] Thibaut's *Vedánta-Sútras*, Vol. I, p. 235. [2] *Ibid*, Vol. II. pp. 149, 150, 152.

Hindu ideas of personality are vague. Fisher says:

"Belief in the personality of man and belief in the personality of God stand or fall together. A glance at the history of religion would suggest that these two beliefs are for some reason inseparable. When faith in the personality of God is weak, or is altogether wanting, as in the case of the pantheistic religions of the East, the perception which men have of their own personality is found to be, in an equal degree, indistinct. The feeling of individuality is dormant. The soul indolently ascribes to itself a merely phenomenal being. It conceives of itself as appearing for a moment, like a wavelet on the ocean, to vanish again in the all-ingulfing essence whence it emerged."[1]

In the Vishnu Purána[2] Nidágha is represented as standing afar off, waiting till a prince should enter the city.

"Tell me," said Ribhu, "which is here the king, and which is any other man." "The king," answered Nidágha, "is he who is seated on the elephant; the others are his attendants." "Tell me, venerable sir, which is the king and which is the elephant?" "The elephant," answered Nidágha, "is underneath, the king is above him." To this Ribhu rejoined, "What is meant by *underneath*, and what is termed *above*?" Upon this Nidágha jumped upon Ribhu and said, "I am above like the Raja; you are underneath like the elephant." "Very well," said Ribhu, "tell me which of us two is *you*; which is *I*?"

"When Nidágha heard these words, he immediately fell at the feet of the stranger and said, 'Of a surety, thou art my saintly preceptor Ribhu; the mind of no other person is so fully imbued with the doctrine of unity as that of my teacher.'"

It is looked upon as profound wisdom not to know "which is *you*, which is *I*?" Ribhu has apparently been incarnated in Professor Deussen. In his *Elements of Metaphysics* he says:—

"You shall love your neighbour as yourselves—because you are your neighbour, and mere illusion makes you believe that your neighbour is something different from yourselves." p. 336.

The absurdity of this will be noticed under another head. The vagueness of the Hindu idea of personality is shown by the belief that the same *átman* may successively be associated with a god, a man, a dog, a musquito, or even a plant.

The following are some of the arguments in favour of belief in a personal God:

1. *"The fact of the universality, or at least the extreme generality, of the belief, in an elementary form."*

Prayer is an instinctive belief in a personal God, and it is universal except among a few who have adopted the dogma of an Impersonal God. Guizot, the great French statesman, eloquently says:

"Alone of all beings here below, man prays! Among his moral instincts none is more natural, more universal, more indestructible than

[1] Fisher's *Grounds of Theistic and Christian Belief*, p. 1.

[2] Book II. Chap. 16.

prayer. The child inclines to it with eager docility. The old man betakes himself thither, as to refuge against decay and solitude. Prayer comes spontaneously to young lips which with difficulty stammer out the name of God, and to dying lips which no longer have strength to pronounce it. Among all nations, celebrated or obscure, civilised or barbarous, one meets at every step acts and forms of invocation. Wherever men live, in certain circumstances, at certain times, under the control of certain impressions of the soul the eyes are raised, the hands clasped, the knees bent to implore aid or render thanks, to adore or to appease. With transport or with fear, publicly or in the secrecy of his heart, it is to prayer that man betakes himself, in the last resort to fill up the void of his soul, or to bear the burdens of his destiny; it is in prayer that he seeks, when all else fails, strength for his weakness, consolation in his grief, hope in his virtue."

Prayer would be useless addressed to a Being unconscious even of its own existence; hence the Vedánta nowhere inculcates it as a duty. In this it contradicts a natural instinct.

2. *The argument from Evidences of Design in the world.* 'Do you not think,' asks Socrates, "that man's Maker must have given him eyes on purpose that he might see'? with the suggested inference that the existence of eyes must be proof of a purposeful Creator. This argument, from the date of its first appearance in Greek philosophy, has been one of the strongest supports of natural theology in the ordinary mind. It has had a long controversial history; but none of the objections raised against it have really differed from those which Aristotle saw and answered in his day."[1]

Some think that it has been weakened by the Darwinian doctrine of evolution; but Huxley admits that it leaves the argument where it found it.

3. *The Moral Argument.*—This consists in the fact that we are conscious of being free, and yet under the obligation of a moral law which can only be conceived as emanating from a personal Author.[2]

Sin is viewed as not only the breach of a law, but also of disobedience to a person. "'Against Thee only have I sinned and done this evil in Thy sight,' has been the cry of religion the whole world over."[3]

Existence in a dreamless sleep may be the highest ideal of the Supreme Deity with persons who regard existence as a curse, but not with others. The Christian belief is that God is not only self-conscious, but cognizant of whatever takes place throughout the vast universe which He has created. He also possesses infinite wisdom, exerted for the benefit of His creatures.

"Pantheism," says Flint "under pretence of exalting God above all categories of thought and existence, reduces Him to the level of dead things, of necessary processes, of abstract ideas,

---

[1] *Personality, &c.* pp. 93, 94. [2] *Ibid*, p. 103. [3] *Ibid*, p. 121.

or even to the still lower level of the unknowable and non-existent."[1]

There must therefore be "a personal God, a Being whose mode of existence is indeed beyond our power to conceive; but who, in however transcendent a manner, thinks, wills, loves, and holds personal intercourse with persons."[2]

Brahma is often defined as *Sat, Chit, Ananda.* These will be considered in turn.

Sat.—The term denotes *simple existence.* Upon this the late Ramachandra Bose remarks:

"God (Brahma) is the Pure Being of some schools of Greek philosophy; but as according to no less a philosopher than Hegel. *Pure Being equals nothing,* He is a non-entity. Ancient philosophy laboured, not only in India, but in all famous centres of speculative thought to reduce God to nothing; and such phrases as the 'Eternal Void' 'the everlasting Night,' etc., were most ingeniously invented to set forth His real nothingness under a cloud of high-sounding words. And modern philosophers are simply following their example in their attempts to maintain the nothingness of God behind an array of imposing technicalities. According to them, God is the Absolute and the Unconditioned. If these technical expressions mean anything, they represent God as Pure Being and nothing more—that subtile, impalpable nonetity which defies every attempt to determine it or give it some definite shape."[3]

Dr. Murray Mitchell says: "Instead of *existence,* it would be more precise to say, *that which exists,* or *an existing thing.*"[4]

Chit.—Intelligence, Gough thus explains the term:

"If we are to use the language of European philosophy, we must pronounce the Brahman of the Upanishads to be *unconscious,* for consciousness begins where duality begins.

"Brahma is not intelligence in our sense of the word. The Indian philosophers everywhere affirm that Brahman *is* knowledge, not that Brahman *has* knowledge; that this knowledge is without an object known, and that omniscience is predicable of Brahman only by a metaphor. If we were to misinterpret such knowledge by the word 'consciousness,' we should still have to say that Brahma *is* consciousness, not that Brahman *has* consciousness or is a conscious spirit. Brahman is the pure light of characterless knowledge."[5]

"Intelligence or thought," says Thibaut, "is not to be predicated of Brahman as its attribute, but constitutes its substance; Brahma is not a thinking being, but thought itself."[6]

Nehemiah Goreh says, "The so-called knowledge of Brahma is *nirvishaya,* objectless, that is, it is not a knowledge of anything, and is therefore no knowledge at all."[7]

---

[1] *Anti-Theistic Theories,* p. 387. [2] Illingworth, p. 211.
[3] *Hindu Philosophy,* pp. 368, 369. [4] *Hinduism,* p. 51.
[5] *Philosophy of the Upanishads,* pp. 41, 42. [6] Introduction to *Vedánta-Sútras,* p. xxv. [7] *Indian Church Quarterly Review,* April 1891, p. 163.

Dr. Murray Mitchell says that the Vedánta doctrine on this point is self-contradictory:

"Where knowledge exists, there must be a knower, and also something known, knowledge being the relation between the two. But the Vedánta explicitly denies that there is such a distinction."[1]

"In Brahma there is no consciousness such as is denoted by 'I,' 'thou,' and 'it;' It apprehends no person or thing nor is apprehended by any." "If Brahma were conscious, there would be objects of consciousness, which would involve dualism; for 'wherever there is consciousness there is relation, and wherever there is relation there is dualism.'"

Nehemiah Goreh says:

"The Vedántists do not hold that the pure spirit, Brahma, really cognizes objects; that is to say, they do not allege that the pure spirit, cognizes objects in this manner 'This is a jar,' 'This is a web,' &c. For if they allowed this sort of cognition to him, they would have to allow to him will, activity, happiness, misery, and so forth; and as a consequence, he would be a doer of good and of evil works, an heir of Elysium or of Hell, and a partaker of three fold pain."[2]

Ananda.—Gough describes it as "Bliss without self-gratulation, bliss in which there is nothing that rejoices and nothing rejoiced at; the unspeakable blessedness of exemption from vicissitude and misery."[3]

"Bliss," says Deussen, "is only a negative quality, and is regarded simply as absence of pain which alone befits Brahma; for, What is different from Him is full of pain."[4]

Col. Jacob says:

"This has been characterised as 'a bliss without the fruition of happiness,' and rightly so. For absorption into Brahma is described as a permanent state, 'resembling precisely that of deep sleep,'—'a condition of insensibility,'—in which the emancipated spirit is without a body, mind, or cognition! Where is there any room in such a state for joy? 'But what, in that case,' says the author of the *Sánkhya-pravachana-bháshya*, 'becomes of the scripture which lays down that the soul' is happiness? The answer is, Because of there being *cessation of misery*, only in a loose acceptation does the term happiness denote soul. . . To move ambition in the dull or ignorant, the emancipated state, which really is *stoppage of misery*, Soul itself, is lauded to them by the Vedas as happiness.' Brahma, then, as joy, is wholly a product of the imagination."[5]

Besides *Sat, Chit, Ánanda,* two other attributes of Brahma may be noticed.

Indivisibility.—In the *Vedánta-Súra* Brahma is described as *Akhanda,* without parts. It is argued that if Brahma were made

---

[1] *Letters on the Evidences of Christianity,* p. 191.
[2] *Rational Refutation, &c.* p. 154.
[3] *Philosophy of the Upanishads,* pp. 36, 37.
[4] *Short Account, &c.* p. 5.
[5] *Hindu Pantheism,* pp. 5, 6.

up of parts, it would follow that It was non-eternal.[1] Sankara says, "We admit Brahman to be without parts just because Scripture reveals it."[2] "Brahma," says Jacob, "is an absolute and unchangeable unity."[3] It follows from this that each individual soul is the complete indivisible Brahma!

Sankara explains that the apparent division of Brahma is only a mere fiction of Ignorance:

"By a break of that nature a thing is not really broken up into parts, not any more than the moon is really multiplied by appearing double to a person of defective vision. By that element of plurality which is the fiction of Ignorance, which is characterised by name and form, which is evolved as well as non-evolved, which is not to be defined either as the existing or the non-existing, Brahma becomes the basis of this entire apparent world with its changes, and so on, while in its true and real nature it at the same time remains unchanged, lifted above the phenomenal universe."[4]

Individual souls, according to Sankara, are only like the reflections of the sun seen in pots of water: they have no real existence.

Unchangeableness.—This is implied in the epithets *nirvikára, kútastha.* Nehemiah Goreh thus notices a common error:

"I warn my readers against being misled by the notions, so prevalent among the vulgar, that, according to the Vedánta, Brahma was once void of qualities, and then, assuming them made the world; and that some small portion of the pure Brahman parted from him, got deluded by illusion and then became souls; which souls, when they free themselves from illusion, will be united to Brahma; &c., &c. The teachers of the Vedánta do not allege that Brahma was once void of qualities, and subsequently, taking them upon him, formed the universe; but they allege, that to be without them has ever distinguished him, and ever will distinguish him."[5]

The above is confirmed by Sankara in the Vedánta-Sútras:

"A number of scriptural passages by denying all modifications of Brahma teach it to be absolutely changeless, (*Kútastha*)....To the one Brahman the two qualities of being subject to modification and of being free from it cannot both be ascribed. But if you say, 'Why should they not be both predicated of Brahma (the former during the time of the subsistence of the world, the latter during the period of re-absorption) just as rest and motion may be predicated (of one body at different times)?' We remark that the qualification 'absolutely changeless' (*Kútastha*) precludes this. For the changeless Brahma cannot be the substratum of varying attributes."[6]

---

[1] *Vedánta-Sútras*, Vol. I. 350.
[2] *Ibid*, p. 350.
[3] *Hindu Pantheism*, p. 6
[4] *Vedánta-Sútras*, Vol. I. p. 352.
[5] *Rational Refutation*, p. 137.
[6] *Vedánta-Sútras*, Vol. I. p. 327.

Moral and Religious Objections to the Vedantic Brahma.

1. **Utter Selfishness is the highest Vedantic Ideal.**—The *prayojana*, or end, set forth in the Vedánta is *liberation*, freedom from the miseries of *samsára*, the attainment of a state of dreamless sleep. The last stage prescribed by Hinduism is to retire to the desert. The hermit is to care only for himself. He is not to give the young the benefit of his experience, he is not to feed the hungry, instruct the ignorant, visit the sick, comfort the sorrowing, extend a helping hand to those struggling in the ocean of life; he is to care only for himself. It must be confessed that in this he is simply imitating Brahma, in whom the doctrine reaches its full development.

The rise of Hindu Pessimism has been described (p. 5). Labour was a burden in a hot climate, and undisturbed repose seemed the highest bliss. This feeling was intensified by the wars that prevailed, but chiefly by the belief in transmigration. The Jews of old were thus addressed by God, "Thou thoughtest that I was altogether such an one as thyself." The Hindus imagined a Brahma after their own heart. He may be compared to a Hindu Raja who spends his life in sloth within his palace, heedless of what is going on throughout his dominions, and leaving everything to his ministers.

"Unencumbered by the cares of empire," says Dr. Duff, "or the functions of a superintending providence, he effectuates no good, inflicts no evil, suffers no pain. He exists in a state of undisturbed repose—a sleep so deep as never to be disturbed by a dream—even without any consciousness of his own existence."

The more a man resembles Brahma, the more selfish and useless he becomes.

Contrast the foregoing with the Christian conception of God. He is the self-existent, the unchanging God, "the same yesterday, to-day, and for ever." He called the universe into being, and His government extends over all creation. He is never unconscious. He never slumbers nor sleeps. "The Creátor of the ends of the earth fainteth not, nor is weary." He knows everything that takes place throughout His vast dominions. Every thought of our heart is known to Him. His ear is ever open to the cry of His children. His character is expressed in the words, "Thou art good and doest good;" "God is love." Still, it is not the feeling which looks upon good and evil with equal eye. If a king allowed crime to go unpunished, his kingdom would become like a hell.

The proverb has been quoted 'As is the god, so is the worshipper.' It will hereafter be shown that Vedantism, tested by its fruits, is found wanting, that the belief in a supposed Brahma has had a tendency to discountenance philanthropic effort. On the other hand, every encouragement has been given to it by the Christian conception of God. It is admitted that sad evils prevail among nations nominally Christian, but among them and them alone are there systematic agencies to combat them. There are Peace Societies to discourage war, there are Red Cross Societies to look after the wounded in battle; there are Societies for the Poor, the Blind, the Deaf and Dumb, the Aged, the Orphan, the Widow, for almost every benevolent object.

2. **The Vedantic Conception of Brahma stifles Religion.**—Love, prayer, worship are three great elements of religion: Vedantism destroys them all.

Miss Waldo, a lecturer on Vedantism in America, admits that "Brahman is too much of an abstraction to be thought of—far more to be loved." "The Vedantic God," says *The Hindu*, "is a cold dreary philosophic conception which the Hindu masses have never cared for, which the vast majority of mankind can never be brought to reverence, and which is quite incapable of influencing them in the formation of life and character."[1]

Thibaut says:

> "The only religious books of wide-spread influence are such as the Rámáyan of Tulsidás, which lay no stress on the distinction between an absolute Brahman inaccessible to all human wants and sympathies, and a shadowy Lord whose very conception depends on the illusory principle of Máyá, but love to dwell on the delights of devotion to one all-wise and merciful Ruler, who is able and willing to lend a gracious ear to the supplication of the worshipper."[2]

Love to God is the very essence of religion. This feeling cannot exist towards a being like Brahma.

"If Vedantism be true," says the Rev. T. E. Slater, "then *prayer*—the universal religion where men of every creed can meet at the feet of a heavenly Father—and *worship*—the noblest activities of the soul must be abandoned."[3] Tennyson well says:

> "For what are men better than sheep or goats
> That nourish a blind life within the brain,
> If, knowing God, they lift not hands of prayer
> Both for themselves and those who call them friend?"

It is useless to address in prayer or worship a God unconscious even of its own existence. The same truths are thus set forth by Professor Flint:

> "Religion supposes faith, love, hope; but pantheism when it denies the personality of God refuses to these affections an appropriate object. It withholds from the view of the spirit what can alone satisfy its best and deepest feelings. The less of determinate personal character God is regarded as having, the less is it possible to love or trust Him.[4]
>
> "The mystical piety of India, when strictly pantheistic, knows nothing of the gratitude for Divine mercy and the trust in Divine

[1] *Brahmavádin*, Vol. II. p. 141. [2] Introduction to *Vedánta-Sútras*, p. cxxviii.
[3] Quoted by Rev. T. E. Slater, *Studies in the Upanishads*, p. 19.
[4] *Anti-Theistic Theories*, pp. 61, 62.

righteousness which characterise evangelical piety. Instead of love and communion in love, it can only commend to us the contemplation of an object which is incomprehensible, devoid of all affections, and indifferent to all actions. When feelings like love, gratitude, and trust are expressed in the hymns and prayers of Hindu worship, it is in consequence of a virtual denial of the principles of pantheism; it is because the mind has consented to regard as real what it had previously pronounced illusory, and to personify what it had declared to be impersonal. Hinduism holds it to be a fundamental truth that the absolute Being can have no personal attributes, and yet it has not only to allow but to encourage its adherents to invest that Being with these attributes, in order that by thus temporarily deluding themselves they may evoke in their hearts at least a feeble and transient glow of devotion. It has even been forced, by its inability to elicit and sustain a religious life by what is strictly pantheistic in its doctrine, to crave the help of polytheism, and to treat the foulest orgies and cruellest rites of idolatry as acts of reasonable worship paid indirectly to the sole and supreme Being. It finds polytheism to be the indispensable supplement of its pantheism. It is the personal gods of Hindu polytheism, and not the impersonal principle of Hindu pantheism, that the Hindu people worship. No people can worship what they believe to be entirely impersonal. Even in the so-called religions of nature the deified natural powers are always personified. It is only as persons that they are offered prayers and sacrifices."

The pernicious effects of pantheism on Indian polytheism are thus shown by Professor Flint:

"I have said that the ability of pantheism to ally itself with polytheism accounts for its prevalence in certain lands; but I must add that although a power, this ability is not a merit. It is a power for evil—power which sustains superstition, corrupts the system which possesses it, deludes and degrades the human mind and heart, and arrests social progress. Educated Hindus are often found to represent it is an excellence of Brahmanism, that it not only tolerates but embraces and incorporates the lower phases of religion. They contend that it thereby elevates and purifies polytheism, and helps the mind of men to pass from the lowest stage of religious development gradually up to the highest. The opinion may seem plausible, but neither reason nor experience confirms it. Pantheism can give support to polytheism and receive support from it, but only at the cost of sacrificing all its claims to be a rational system, and of losing such moral virtue as it possesses. If it look upon the popular deities as mere fictions of the popular mind, its association with polytheism can only mean a conscious alliance with falsehood, the deliberate propagation of lies, a persistent career of hypocrisy . . . India alone is surely sufficient proof that the union of pantheism with polytheism does not correct but stimulate the extravagances of the latter. Pantheism, instead of elevating and purifying Hindu polytheism, has contributed to increase the number, the absurdity, and the foulness of its superstitions."[1]

It has already been shown that Vedántism cuts the roots of morality.

---

[1] *Anti-Theistic Theories*, pp. 386-391 abridged.

ISVARA.

Brahma is said to exist in two conditions—*nirguna*, unbound, and *saguna*, bound. The two states are sometimes called the Higher and Lower Brahmá. The former is called Brahma, neuter; the latter Brahmá, masculine. The name I'śvara, lord, is also often applied to the latter.

Brahma *nirguna*, as already mentioned, exists in a state of dreamless sleep, unconscious of its own existence. It is a common error to imagine that the *nirguna* Brahma, assuming qualities, made the world. According to the Vedánta the *nirguna* Brahma never changes, never acquires qualities. The *saguna* Brahma consists of Brahma associated with ignorance—a union which is said to be eternal.

The Brahmá of the Puranas and the Brahmá of Vedántism are two very different beings. Each will be noticed in turn.

Brahma of the Puranas.—The sacred books of the Hindus give conflicting accounts of the origin of Brahmá, the first of the Hindu triad. The *Satapatha Bráhmana* says that at first nothing but water existed. The waters performed austerities and produced the golden egg from which Brahmá, called Prajápatí, arose. The same Bráhmana elsewhere represents the gods as the creators of Prajápatí. The Mahábhárata asserts that Brahmá sprang from the navel of Vishnu or from a lotus which grew thereout. His five heads are said to have arisen from lusting after his daughter. Siva cut off one of them with the thumb of his left hand. Very contradictory accounts are given of creation by Brahmá. He was afterwards married to Sarasvatí, and had a heaven of his own, called Brahma or Satya loka.

Brahma or Isvara in the Vedanta.—The description given of him by some of the foremost Orientalists will first be quoted:

"Brahma," says Colonel Jacob, "is illusorily associated with three kinds of bodies:

"*Firstly*, with a causal body, composed of Ignorance or Illusion, which in the aggregate is I'śvara, or god, and distributively, individual souls or Prájna. It is likened to a state of dreamless sleep.

"*Secondly*, with a subtile body composed of the five organs of sense and of action, mind, intellect, and the five vital airs, seventeen in all. This, in the aggregate, is called Hiranyagarbha, or the Thread Soul, and, in the distributed state, Taijasa. It is likened to a state of dream.

"*Thirdly*, with a gross body, composed of the compound elements. Viewed in the aggregate, it is called Vaiśvánara, and, distributively, Viśva. It is likened to the waking state.

"A fourth state is that of the unassociated pure Brahma which is technically styled 'The Fourth.'[1]

---

[1] *Hindu Pantheism*, p. 74.

Gough gives further details regarding I'svara's three emanations:

Isvara not a personal God but the universal soul.—Gough says:

"This conception of the world-projecting deity is not theistic. He is nothing else than the totality of souls in dreamless sleep, present in the heart of every living thing; himself only the first figment of the world-fiction; resolved into the characterless unity of Brahman, at the close of each age of the world, and issuing out of that unity at each *palingenesia* (second birth) in the eternal procession of the æons. He is eternal, but every migrating soul is co-eternal with him, a co-eternal and only equally fictitious emanation of the one and only self. He can hardly be conceived to have any separate personality apart from the souls he permeates and vivifies; and his state is not one of consciousness, but that of the pure bliss of dreamless sleep. One with the sum of living beings in that state, he is yet said to allot to each of them their portion of weal and woe, but only in accordance with their merits in prior forms of embodied existence....I'śvara is no less unreal than the migrating soul; and both I'śvara and the soul are only so far existent as they are fictitious manifestations of the one and only Self."

"**Hiranyagarbha, the spirit of dreaming sentiencies.**—The next emanation in the order of descent is Hiranyagarbha, Práṇa, the Thread-spirit. This divine emanation is the totality of migrating souls in the state of dreaming sleep, the sum of the dreaming consciousness of the world. His body is the sum of the invisible bodies, the tenuous *involucra* (wrappers, sheaths) clothed in which the soul passes from body to body in the long process of metempsychosis. These invisible bodies are made up of three vestures one upon the other, the cognitional, the sensorial, and the aërial garments of soul. These three wrappers clothe Hiranyagarbha (the embryo of light.) He is called *Sútrátma*, the Thread-spirit, as stringing together all dreaming souls clothed in the invisible bodies that accompany them in their migrations, as pearls are strung upon a thread to form a necklace.

"**Viraj, the spirit of waking sentiencies.**—The third and lowest of the progressive emanations is Viraj, Vaiśvánara, Prajápatí, or Purusha. His body is the whole mundane egg, the outer shell of the visible world, or the sum of the visible and perishing bodies of migrating souls. He is identified with the totality of waking consciousness, with the sum of souls in the waking state and the sum of their gross visible and tangible environments. He is the sum of souls that illusively identify themselves with their outer bodies, and thus suffer hunger, thirst and faintness. and all the other miseries of metempsychosis."[1]

Subdivisions of Isvara.—These are described at great length in the Vedánta Sára (See pp. 29-36). Some of the points have already been noticed. R. C. Bose says:

"Every soul is, according to the Vedántic system, a synthesis (compound) of a particle of Ignorance and a particle of Brahman invaria-

[1] *Philosophy of the Upanishads*, abridged, pp. 55-58.

bly called Intelligence. Every soul therefore represents Ignorance in its distributive form or as a distributive aggregate. The Ignorances attached to the innumerable souls in the world emanated from and are to be re-absorbed in one mass of Ignorance, called 'Collective Ignorance.' This Collective Ignorance or totality of Ignorance, is called I'śvara or God, the Creator and Preserver and Destroyer of the world. It is, however, not appropriately called I'śvara, for it forms only the 'causal body' of this Being. I'śvara, like the individual soul, is a synthesis, and consists of the compound of all Ignorances, called Collective Ignorance, and a very large portion of Brahma, the sum total of all the particles of Brahma attached to the innumerable souls in the world. Collective Ignorance is, therefore, his causal body rather than his entire self. Distributive Ignorance is in the same way the 'causal body' of the individuated soul, and not its entire self. The relationship between Collective Ignorance and Distributive Ignorance is illustrated in the Vedánta-Sára by that subsisting between a 'forest' and 'the trees' of which it consists, or that between 'a lake' and 'the waters' of which it consists.

"A thing is regarded as a collective or distributive aggregate according as it is viewed as a whole or as a collection of parts."

"But these divisions and subdivisions of Brahma into innumerable parts, associated to various spheres of existence and various classes of objects, subtle and gross, cannot but suggest the idea of dualism. How is the integrity of monism to be maintained in the teeth of descriptions so obviously at war with it? To understand this it is necessary to comprehend the Vedántic notion of 'erroneous imputations' (*adhyáropa*) and its 'refutation.'[1]

'Erroneous Imputation' is the allegation that the Unreal is the Real—like the judgment in respect of a rope which is no serpent, that it is a serpent.

"The 'Real' is Brahma, existence, knowledge, and happiness, without a second; the 'Unreal' is the whole aggregate of the senseless—beginning with Ignorance."[2]

"Brahma is *real*, absolute, unconditioned, unrelated existence, without consciousness, without feeling, without qualities. But in all ordinary descriptions of Brahma certain attributes and operations are attributed to him. He is represented as omnipotent and omniscient, as creator and preserver, as associated to various spheres of existence and various classes of objects, as enslaved by and emancipated from ignorance. But the representations by which he is set forth as conditioned and related, determined by qualities, states and acts, are all 'false,' knowingly resorted to by the learned for the purpose of making the absolute intelligible to the unlearned."[3]

Gough has the following remarks on the same subject:

"**Isvara passes into seeming plurality.**—It is through the union from before all time of Brahma with the inexplicable illusion, that the one and only self presents itself in the endless plurality and diversity of transient deities, of migrating spirits, and of the worlds through which they migrate. It is through this union that

[1] "Illusory Attribution." "Withdrawal," Jacob. [2] *Vedántá Sára.*
[3] B. C. Bose, *Hindu Philosophy*, pp. 350, 351.

the one and only Self is present in every creature, as one and the same ether is present in many water-jars, as one and the same sun is mirrored in countless sheets of water. It is through this union that the one and only Self permeates and animates the world. In the words of Sankara: 'The image of the sun upon a piece of water expands with the expansion, and contracts with the contraction, of the ripples on the surface; moves with the motion, and is severed by the breaking of the ripples. The reflection of the sun thus follows the various conditions of the surface, but not so the real sun in the heavens. It is in a similar manner that the real Self is reflected upon its counterfeits, the bodies of sentient creatures, and thus fictitiously limited, shares their growth and diminution, and other sensible modes of being. Apart from its various counterfeits, the Self is changeless and unvaried.[1] The one and only Self is present in the heart of every living one as one and the same face may be reflected by a succession of mirrors."[2]

REMARKS ON I'SVARA.

As already mentioned, the false dogma was assumed by the Vedánta that Brahma alone exists, "One without a second." As this was contradicted by the evidence of the senses, and the experience of the whole human race, it was sought to be supported by another invented dogma, *Avidyá,* Ignorance. It has been shown that Avidyá is a mere fiction to bolster up another error.

In the Purânas the highest gods are charged with crimes which would disgrace a human being. In the Vedánta almost equal dishonour is done to God by eternally associating Ignorance with Him, whereas God, the Great Creator and Lord of the universe, is possessed of unbounded knowledge and wisdom. 'God is light; in Him is no darkness at all.'

The doctrines of Avidyá and the three emanations of I'śvara which have been described are altogether destitute of proof. They are like the other wild speculations of the Hindu sacred books about the human body, geography, and astronomy. Intelligent Hindus will allow that the disgraceful stories told about Brahmá in the Purânas are fictions, proceeding from a wicked filthy imagination. The Vedántic speculations about I'śvara are equally baseless.

According to the Vedánta-Sára, I'śvara is the collective aggregate of all animated beings, from the highest deities down to a blade of grass, just as a forest is a collective aggregate of trees. Upon this Colonel Jacob remarks:

"This, to any ordinary mind, is tantamount to saying there is no personal God at all; for how can it be supposed that this aggregate of

[1] Introduction to *Svetásvatara Upanishad.*

[2] *Philosophy of the Upanishads,* pp. 49, 50.

sentiencies has, or has ever had, any power of united action, so as to constitute it a personal Being? Yet, after describing God as identical with the aggregate of individual sentiencies, apart from which he can have no more existence than a forest can have apart from the trees which compose it, the text proceeds to treat him as a personal Being, endowed with the qualities of omniscience, &c., and bearing rule over individual souls!

"The attributes assigned to him are thus explained by the commentator. His *omniscience* is merely his being a witness of the whole universe, animate and inanimate. He is called 'I'śvara,' because he presides over individual souls and allots rewards according to their works. How this aggregate of individual souls is to preside over itself and reward each soul included in it according to its works, it is impossible to say; but his functions in this capacity ought to be a sinecure, inasmuch as it is strongly insisted upon that works, whether good or bad, are followed by an exactly proportioned measure of reward or punishment without the intervention of anybody. He is the '*controller*' in the sense of being the mover or impeller of souls; and the '*internal ruler*' as dwelling in the heart of each, and restraining the intellect. He is the '*cause of the world*,' not as its creator, but as the seat of the evolution of that illusory effect. Indeed, it would be inconsistent to speak of a creator of a world which has no greater reality than belongs to things seen in a dream!" [1]

"The so-called personal God, the first manifestation of the Impersonal, turns out on examination to be a myth." [2]

I's'wara, in reality, is a non-entity. Nehemiah Goreh says:

"The Vedánta recognizes, as existent, an I'śwara, maker of the world, all-wise, and all-powerful; and souls, also, and their ignorance, their doing good and evil, their requital in Elysium and in Hell, and their transmigration. And, again, all these are regarded as non-existent, and as absolutely so. Neither are they, nor have they been, nor are they to be. Brahma alone exists,—without qualities, and eternal. All besides—I's'wara, the world, and everything else,—has but a false existence, and owes its being to imagination by ignorance. In very truth, it is nothing. Such, in a few words, is the creed of the Vedántins." [3]

CREATION.

According to Hinduism, there is no creation in the strict sense of the word. This is the result of that fixed dogma of a Hindu philosopher's belief—*návastuno vastusiddhih,* nothing can be produced out of nothing.

The Rev. Nehemiah Goreh thus states the case:—

"By the word Creator, Christians as well as Theists mean one who gave being to things which had no being before, or according to the phrase used in Christian Theology, created things out of nothing. In

[1] *Hindu Pantheism*, pp. 58, 59. [2] *Hindu Pantheism*, p. 129.
[3] *Rational Refutation*, p. 126.

this sense no sect of religion or school of philosophy among the Hindus believes God to have created anything.

"And here I wish to say that such of our countrymen as have been educated in English schools and colleges, and are not familiar with the true tenets of Hinduism are apt to be misled by certain words and phrases used in the religious books of our country. They are apt to think that those words and phrases were used by the authors of those books and are understood by orthodox Hindus, in the same sense which they themselves attach to them, having acquired more enlightened notions of religious truths by coming in contact with Christianity, and then to think that those very notions are taught in those books. For instance it is stated in those books that God is *Sarva-kartá*, that is, maker of all. Yet it would be a great mistake to think that they teach that God is the *Creator* of all things. It is a fixed principle with the teachers of all the schools of philosophy in our country (and remember that with the Hindus philosophy is religion and religion is philosophy) that every *Kárya*, that is, effect, must have a *Samaváyi* or *Upádána Kárana*, that is, a cause out of which an effect is produced or formed, such as clay is to an earthen pot. It may be translated by the English word 'material cause' in some cases though not in all. Therefore the world could not be created out of nothing. According to the Hindus' belief the world has an *Upádána Kárana*, or a material cause, and that material cause is uncreated, self-existing, and eternal like God Himself. According to the Nyáya school, the *paramánus*, or atoms of earth, water, fire, and air, which are infinite in number, are the material cause of visible and tangible parts of this universe, and are themselves self-existent and eternal. Moreover *A'kása*, time, space, souls, not only of men, but also of gods, animals, and plants, and *manas*, the internal organs which together with souls are infinite in number, are all uncreated, self-existent, and eternal. Very little indeed have they left for God to do. He only frames, with these self-existent substances, the world. According to the Sánkhya system *prakriti* is the material cause of the universe, and it is of course self-existent and eternal.

"Even the false god of the Vedántists, the maker of the false world, is only a framer of it like the God of the Nyaya, and not a *Creator*, Máyá being the *Upádána Kárana*, or material cause of it. From this Máyá, though false yet eternal, the whole universe is evolved, as according to the Sánkhya it is evolved from their eternal *prakriti*." [1]

It has been stated that the fundamental error of Hinduism is to judge by our own standard. A carpenter cannot work without materials; in like manner it is supposed that God must have formed all things from eternally existing matter. The fallacy of this is thus shown by the late Rev. Dr. K. M. Banerjea:

"That no man can work without materials is denied by none, simply because man is not omnipotent, and has not creative power. But when one looks at an exquisite production of art, he is so lost in admiration at the skill of the artist, that he almost forgets the minor question of the material. And yet so banefully has the theory of material causality

---

[1] *Theism and Christianity*, Part I. pp. 5-7.

worked among us that the mental energy of our philosophers has found most active exercise NOT *in the exclamation*, How wonderful is the arrangement of the universe! BUT in the interrogation, Of what pre-existing substance is all this made? Nay they have been so lost in that question, as to forget that a Creator of infinite power and perfection needs not, like weak and imperfect man, to stop for materials, but can make materials by the mere *fiat* of His will. If the natural instincts of the human soul lead us to believe in the existence of an all-powerful and perfect Being, if the irresistible arguments of the Vedánta itself drive us to the conclusion that the universe was created by a God, infinite in wisdom and contrivance; then there can be no possible necessity for speculating on the *material* of the world: then the most philosophical course is to consider the object originally created by such a God as at once the *matter and form* of the world. To assume the eternity of some gross material, existing side by side with an intelligent and all-perfect God, is not only unnecessary (and therefore unphilosophical,) inasmuch as it assumes two principles, where one is amply sufficient to account for all we see; but it is inconsistent with the idea of perfection which we must attribute to the Deity. If he had some material to work upon, previously existing independent of Him, then there was nothing peculiar in His agency; then it was of the same species as that of a human architect; then he was our creator in no higher sense than that in which a potter is the maker of a jar. The Vedántist, on the other hand, places himself in a false position, by seeking in a spiritual essence, the substance of such a world, consisting of pure and impure, intelligent, and unintelligent, rational and irrational, animated and inanimated creatures."

"Ye do err, not knowing the power of God," applies to Hindus as well as those to whom the words were addressed by the Great Teacher. Even the *Brahmavádín* makes the acknowledgment:

"He, in whom all things in the universe live and move and have their being possesses potentialities inscrutable to human wisdom and capable of infinite and very wonderful manifestations." Aug. 29, 1897.

Whether is it more rational to suppose the eternal existence of one Being, infinite in power and wisdom, or to imagine that innumerable unintelligent atoms and spirits existed from all eternity? Besides the latter, an eternal, intelligent Arranger is also required. Some Vedántic ideas about creation will now be noticed.

Creation ascribed to "mere sport."—The Vedánta-Sútra II., 1-33, is as follows:

"But (Brahman's creative activity) is mere sport such as we see in ordinary life."

On the above S'ankara makes the following comment:

"We see in every-day life that certain doings of princes or other men of high position who have no unfulfilled desires left have no reference to any extraneous purpose, but proceed from mere sportfulness as, for instance, their recreations in places of amusement.... Analogously, the activity of the Lord also may be supposed to be mere sport, proceeding from his own nature, without reference to any purpose."[1]

The Hindu gods are sometimes said to commit sin "in sport or as a divine amusement." With this motive the Small-Pox goddess is said to scatter the seeds of the disease. What degrading conceptions do all these show of the Divine Being!

Contradictory Hindu Accounts of Creation.—Several of these are described in the fourth volume of Muir's *Sanskrit Texts.* Here only a short quotation may be made from Sankara's commentary on the Brahma-Sútras. II. 2, 3.

"The Chhándogya intimates that fire was created first, while the Taittiryaka assigns the same position to ether, and because it is impossible that both should have been created first."[2]

Only one or two of the principal notions on the subject can be examined.

Two Hindu Theories of Creation.—When a potter makes a pot, he is the *operative* cause, while the clay is the *material* or *upádána* cause. Sútras 23-26. I Adhyáya, 4 Páda, *Brahma-Sútras,* hold that Brahma is the *material* cause of the universe, framing it out of himself as a spider evolves its web out of its own body.

The later theory is that *Máyá* is both the *operative* and *material* cause of the world.

The World no Beginning.—The great Hindu problem is to account for the inequalities of life. The solution given is that they arise from merit and demerit in a former birth. To this it is replied that beings must have existed before there could be merit or demerit. Merit and demerit may be compared to a hen, and the body produced to the egg. A hen could not be produced from its own egg. It is argued "that the first creation in the series of creations must have been one of pure equality, there not having yet arisen any such retributive fatality in consequence of a prior variety of embodiment."

The Vedánta Sútras thus reply to this:

"If it be objected that it (viz. the Lord's having regard to merit and demerit) is impossible on account of the non-distinction (of merit and demerit, previous to the first creation); we refute the objection on the ground of (the world) being without a beginning." II. i. 35.

Sankara thus replies to the objection:

"*The series of creations has had no beginning.* Your plea would be good if the series had a beginning, but it has none; and consequently there is nothing to gainsay the position that the law of retribution and the inequalities of life produce and reproduce each other like seed and plant, and plant and seed.

---

[1] Thibaut's Translation, Vol. II. p. 5.

[2] Gough's *Philosophy of the Upanishads*, p. 208.

"You will next ask us, how we know that the series of creations has had no beginning. Our reply is this—that if the series had beginning, something must have come out of nothing. . . . There would no longer be anything to account for the inequalities of happiness and misery in the world."

Sankara thus refutes his own reply:

"This difficulty is not removed by the consideration that the works of living beings and the resulting dispositions made by the Lord form a chain which has no beginning; for in past time as well as in the present mutual interdependence of the two take place, so that the beginningless series is like an endless chain of blind men leading other blind men."[1]

Sankara justly says that the difficulty is not removed by a supposed endless chain—however far back we go, there would be the same impossibility of a hen being produced from its own egg—merit and demerit existing before beings who could originate them.

Sankara starts with the assumption that God cannot create. It has been shown that for this there is no proof; that we cannot judge of the Almighty by comparing him with a carpenter or potter.

The World was formed out of Prakriti or Pradhana.—This is the Sánkhya doctrine, explained at page 10.

Sankara thus replies:

"The origin, &c., of a world possessing the attributes stated above cannot possibly proceed from anything else but a Lord possessing the stated qualities; not either from a non-intelligent pradhána or from atoms, or from non-being, or from a being subject to transmigration; nor again, can it proceed from its own nature (*i.e.*, spontaneously without a cause) since we observe that (for the production of effects) special places, times, and causes have invariably to be employed."[2]

Elsewhere he goes more into detail:

"If you Sánkhyas base your theory on parallel instances merely, we point out that a non-intelligent thing which, without being guided by an intelligent being, spontaneously produces effects capable of subserving the purposes of some particular person is nowhere observed in the world. We rather observe that houses, palaces, couches, pleasure-grounds, and the like,—things which according to circumstances are conducive to the attainment of pleasure or the avoidance of pain—are made by workmen endowed with intelligence. Now look at this entire world which appears, on the one hand, as external (*i.e.*, inanimate) in the form of earth and the other elements enabling (the souls) to enjoy the fruits of their various actions, and, on the other hand, as animate, in the form of bodies which belong to the different classes of beings, possess a definite arrangement of organs, and are therefore capable of constituting the abodes of fruition; look, we say, at this world, of which the most ingenious workmen cannot even form a conception in their minds, and then say if a non-intelligent principle like the *pradhána* is able to fashion it. Other

[1] Thibaut's Translation, Vol. I. p. 435. [2] *Ibid*, Vol. I. pp. 16, 17.

non-intelligent things such as stones and clods of earth are certainly not seen to possess analogous powers. We rather must assume that just as clay and similar substances are seen to fashion themselves into various forms if worked upon by potters and the like, so the *pradhána* also (when modifying itself into its effects) is ruled by some intelligent principle."[1]

By somewhat similar reasoning, Sankara refutes Kanáda's doctrine of atoms:

"As we have shown in our examination of the Sánkhya system, a non-intelligent thing which is not directed by an intelligent principle cannot of itself either act or be the cause of action, and the soul cannot be the guiding principle of the *adrishta* because at the time of *pralaya*, its intelligence has not yet arisen. If, on the other hand, the unseen principle is supposed to inhere in the soul, it cannot be the cause of motion in the atoms, because there exists no connexion of it with the latter. If you say that the soul in which the unseen principle inheres is connected with the atoms, then there would result, from the continuity of connexion, continuity of action, as there is no other restricting principle.—Hence, there being no definite cause of action, original action cannot take place in the atoms; there being no action, conjunction of the atoms which depends on action cannot take place; there being no conjunction, all the effects depending on it; viz., the formation of living atomic compounds, &c., cannot originate."[2]

The reasoning of Sankara in the above quotations cannot be disputed; but he does not see that the same argument equally demolishes his own theory of *Avidyá*, which is practically *prakriti*, or *pradhána*.

Creation is ascribed to Brahma associated with *Avidyá* or *Máyá*. Brahma exists in a state of dreamless sleep; hence the work of creation is due to *avidyá*. The word signifies 'non-knowledge.' *Máyá* likewise, says Thibaut, is of a non-intelligent nature, owing to which it is by so many Vedántic writers identified with the *prakriti* of the Sánkhyas. It may well be asked how can that which is "non-knowledge" frame a world so wonderfully constructed as ours? Sankara's objections to *prakriti*, *pradhána* and atoms apply to *avidyá* or *máyá*.

Hindu Speculations about the Universe.

Speculation instead of Observation.—A so-called Hindu philosopher sat in his house and framed a description of the world out of his own head. In the centre he placed an immense rock, called Meru, 84,000 yojanas in height and 16,000 yojanas below the surface of the earth. Around this mountain he imagined seven continents separated by seven seas of salt water, sugar-cane juice, wine, milk, &c.

---

[1] Thibaut's Translation, Vol. I. pp. 364, 365.
[2] *Vedánta Sútras*, Vol. I. p. 388.

Careful measurement has shown that the Earth is only about 8,000 miles in diameter, so that all the above statements are mere fictions. The same want of observation is shown, though in a less degree, in the statement about the four kinds of bodies, "viviparous, oviparous, moisture-engendered, and germinating." The "moisture-engendered are those produced from moisture as lice, gnats." No creatures are produced from moisture. Lice, gnats, ants, &c., are produced from eggs.

Happily in India a beginning has been made in the right direction. Professor Bose and Dr. Roy, by careful investigation, have been made to command the respect of European scientists.

True Account of Creation.

The Need of a Great First Cause.—The truth of the Sanskrit proverb *návastuno vastusiddhi,* and the Latin proverb *ex nihilo, nihil fit,* 'nothing can be produced out of nothing' is admitted. If ever there had been no existence, there would be no existence still. Nothing cannot make something. Hence, *something has always existed.* Herbert Spencer says,

> "The existence of a first cause of the universe is a necessity of thought. . . . Amid the mysteries which become more mysterious the more they are thought about, there will remain the one absolute certainty that we are ever in the presence of an Infinite, Eternal Energy from which all things proceed."

That which is unconscious and unintelligent cannot will, and cannot act intelligently. Unconscious and unintelligent particles of matter could never arrange themselves into a universe so wonderful as the present. That which has not life cannot give life; that which cannot think cannot form beings with reason. The eternal self-existent First Cause must, therefore, be conscious and intelligent. The acts of a mind prove the existence of a mind; and a mind proves a person.

There is therefore a Self-existent, Eternal, Personal Being, whom wise men reverence and call God.

When it is said that God made all things, it is sometimes asked, Who made God? This is thought to be a proof that there is no Creator. The folly of such an argument can easily be shown by taking a similar case. A person says that a watch must have been made by some wise man. An objector asks, Who made the man? Therefore the watch had no maker!

Buddhists consider that beings are formed by merit and demerit. This does not explain the origin of things. As already explained, creatures must have existed and acted before there could be merit and demerit.

Row says, "I have heard it urged that we must give an account of the origin of this first cause. But if this first cause could be conceived of as itself caused, it would cease to be a first cause; and so we should have to give an account of the origin of this cause, and then of its cause, until we arrived at a first cause, which is itself uncaused."

2. **The Argument from Design.**—Wherever we see order and means intended to accomplish some end, we are certain that they must have originated in the action of an intelligent being.

If on landing on an island, apparently desert and uninhabited, mathematical figures were seen traced on the sand, it would at once be inferred that some person had been there: the figures could not have come by chance. Suppose that on exploring the island further we found a palace, without a human being, but completely furnished with every necessary for the want of man: what would be the conclusion? "Every house is builded by some man."

We know that stones, mortar, wood, and iron, without life or reason, could not have arranged themselves into a house. We are certain, therefore, that the house must have had an intelligent builder. In like manner, we know that the world must have had a wise and powerful Creator.

Cicero, a celebrated Roman writer, says: "If a concourse of atoms can make a world, why not a porch, a temple, a house, a city, which are works of less labour and difficulty?"

In a fine building, each stone is made of a particular shape to suit its future position. Chemistry tells us, that the whole universe is composed of atoms so excessively small that they cannot be seen. It further shows that each atom is, as it were, cast in a fixed mould, so that it will unite with others only in certain proportions. The very atoms therefore, afford irresistible proof that they were fashioned by the great Architect of nature.

If a Designing Mind is denied, we are driven to the absurdity of supposing that all the wonderful arrangements in Nature are the result of chance. As well might the origin of the Rámáyana be ascribed to shaking a large number of letters out of a bag, which grouped themselves into verses, the admiration of the world.

The word *Nature* is sometimes used to express a power, but to deny a personal agent. A disbeliever in the existence of God was once asked how all things around us were produced. He replied, "By Nature." The question was then put, "What is Nature?" The answer was "All around us." So then "*All around us* produced *all around us*!"

Evolution is also given as an explanation. By this is meant that all plants and animals that have ever lived on the earth have come from one simple form into which life was first breathed. Whether this is true or false, it does not supersede the necessity of a Creator. It makes no difference whether He acts in Nature every moment or at once contrived and executed His own part in the plan of the world.

Design does not cease to be design, because the Designer, instead of directly framing plants and animals, made the material in such a way and with such skill as to enable it in the course of ages to run itself, so to speak, into myriad shapes of life and beauty.

Paley shows that if a watch were so constructed that it would produce other watches, this, instead of proving that it had no maker, would only enhance the idea of his skill. Such an arrangement could not have been devised by unconscious matter. In like manner children are not born through the wisdom of their parents.

3. **The wisest men in all ages have acknowledged the existence of a Great Creator, possessed of infinite power and wisdom.**—Socrates, wisest of the Greeks, has an interesting dialogue in support of this truth. Aristotle, a profound Greek philosopher, says, "Although invisible to every mortal nature, God is yet manifested by His works."

Sir Isaac Newton has been called the "Prince of Mathematicians." His Latin treatise, *Principia,* treating of the grand law by which the heavenly bodies are regulated in their movements, is considered the greatest work of the kind which has ever appeared. His conclusion is as follows:

> "This most beautiful system of the sun, planets, and comets, could only proceed from the counsel and dominion of an intelligent and powerful Being."

Lord Kelvin is one of the most distinguished scientific men of the present day. It was through him that the electric telegraph cable was laid across the Atlantic. Addressing some of the most learned men in Europe, he said:—

> "Overpowering proof of intelligence and benevolent design lies around us; and if ever perplexities, whether metaphysical or scientific, turn us away from them for a time, they come back upon us with irresistible force, showing to us, through Nature, the influence of a free-will, and teaching us that all living beings depend upon the ever-acting Creator and Ruler."

The more we know of God's works, the more wonderful they appear. The telescope shows their infinite greatness; the microscope unveils the wisdom with which the smallest creatures are formed.

Every person who reflects seriously must scout the idea that the universe proceeded from an unintelligent cause, called *avidyá* or *máyá,* and must say with Milton:

"These are Thy glorious works, Parent of good,
Almighty! Thine this universal frame,
Thus wondrous fair: Thyself how wondrous then!
Unspeakable, who sit'st above these heavens,
To us invisible, or dimly seen
In these Thy lowest works; yet these declare
Thy goodness beyond thought, and power divine."

MAN: BODY AND SOUL.

THE BODY.

The ancient Hindus thought that a man was rendered impure by touching a dead body. Hence they did not dissect and examine it minutely as is done in modern Medical Colleges. The writers of the Upanishads simply framed an imaginary body out of their own heads, and, to impose upon the ignorant, said that it had been revealed by Brahma.

The following assertion is made in the Chhándogya Upanishad:—

"There are a hundred and one arteries of the heart, one of these penetrates the crown of the head; moving upwards by it a man reaches the immortals; the others serve for departing in different directions, yea, in different directions." VIII. 6. 6.

When the soul proceeds to Brahma, it ascends by the coronal artery, *sushumná*, which springs from the upper part of the heart and goes to the top of the head. This is called the door of rejoicing. When the soul goes out to some other body it proceeds by the other arteries.

Hindu philosophers agree that mind (*manas*) is distinct from spirit or soul. Mind is not eternal in the same way.

It is an internal organ of the body, standing between the four organs of perception and the five organs of action, connected with both, receiving the impressions conveyed by both, and directing both through the exercise of volition. To the mind appertains the faculties of perception (*buddhi*) volition (*sankalpa, vikalpa*), self-consciousness and thought; and the spirit cannot possess these, unless joined to mind and invested with a bodily covering or vehicle.

Monier Williams says:

"Of actual bodily coverings there are three according to the Vedánta system. The causal body (*Kárana-šaríra*) comes first. This is identified with *Ajnána* or *Máyá* and is therefore no real body. Secondly the subtle body, (*linga*, or *súkshma-šaríra*) which encloses a portion of the universal spirit in three sheaths (*kosha*), cognitional, sensorial and aerial, constituting it a living individual personal spirit (*jívátman*) and carrying it through all its corporeal migrations,—till, on its reunion with its source, even its subtle body becomes extinct. Thirdly the gross body (*sthúla-šaríra*), which surrounds the subtle vehicle, and is of various forms in the various conditions of existence through animate or inanimate, organic or inorganic life."[1]

---

[1] *Brahmanism and Hinduism*, pp. 27, 28.

The Soul.

Disparity between Hindu and European Ideas of the Soul.— Crozier says:

"When we Europeans, speak of soul and when the Hindus speak of it, we mean two quite different and indeed opposite things. With us soul is a principle of self-conscious intelligence and will; with the Hindus it is a mere vague diffused essence pervading Nature, the distinctive quality of which is that it is without thought, emotion, will, self-consciousness, or, indeed, any other quality whatever except that of extension and life."[1]

According to Hindu philosophy the same soul may, in different births, be connected with a human being, a beast, fish, insect or even attached to a vegetable or mineral, all the time remaining unconscious. The European idea is that the soul is the great animating and directing principle, the internal ruler, though, alas, it often yields to the bodily appetites.

Some Vedántic dogmas about the soul will now be examined.

The Soul partakes of the attributes of Brahma.—As already explained, Brahma is said to be pure being, unconscious of its own existence, happy simply in being free from the miseries of *samsára*. Its state is described as a dreamless sleep. Practically, it is a nonentity.

The soul may be described as a miniature Brahma.

When we know anything, the Vedántists suppose that it is not the soul that knows, but the *antaḥ-karaṇa*, the internal ruler. "The latter is a sort of inlet of thought, belonging only to the body and existing with it, and quite as distinct from the spirit as any of the external organs of the body."

"The *antaḥ-karaṇa* is divided into *Buddhi*, 'perception'; *Ahankára*, 'self-consciousness'; and *Manas* 'determination'; to which the Vedántists add a fourth division, *Chitta*, 'the thinking or reasoning organ."[2]

The soul being unconscious does not cognize anything. It has always been like a stone, and will ever remain like a stone. It is the *antaḥ-karaṇa* which cognizes.

The Vedántists hold that if cognition belonged to the soul, will, activity, happiness, misery, &c. would follow; the soul would be a doer of good and evil, an experiencer of three-fold misery, whereas the soul is, like Brahma, eternally pure and free. Hence Vedántists ascribe cognition to the *antaḥ-karaṇa*.

2. **The Soul eternal and Svayambhu** (self-existent). Colebrooke says: "The soul is likewise declared expressly to be

[1] *History of Intellectual Development, &c.* p. 86.
[2] Monier Williams, *Indian Wisdom*, pp. 53, 54.

eternal and unborn. Its emanation is no birth, nor original production." The Vedánta-Sútra, II. 3, 17 is as follows:

"The (living) self is not (produced) as there is no scriptural statement, and as it is eternal according to them (*i.e.*, scriptural passages.")

The Katha Upanishad, II. 18, quoted in the Bhagavad Gítá, II. 19, 20, says:

"The wise one (the soul) is not born nor does it die; it was not produced from any one, nor was any produced from it; unborn, eternal, without decay, ancient, it is not slain when the body is slain."

3. **Conflicting Statements about the Size of the Soul.**—Nehemiah Goreh says:

"According to the pandits dimension is of three descriptions; atomic, intermediate, and infinite. Atomic dimension is the last degree of minuteness. Intermediate dimension is that of a jar, &c. However great it may be, it has limits. Infinite dimension the third kind is unlimited. It is this opinion of dimension which, the pandits teach belongs to God, to souls, to ether, to time and to space; and whatever has this dimension is all-pervading. Further, according to them, things of atomic or of infinite dimension are indestructible, but those of intermediate dimension cannot be indestructible. A soul, then, to be indestructible must needs be, in size, either atomic or infinite. If atomic its qualities cannot be cognized; hence the pandits are compelled, on their principles to regard the soul as of infinite dimension."[1]

In the Upanishads the soul is generally said to be of the size of a thumb, and to dwell in the heart. Thus the Katha Upanishad says:

"The soul, which, in the measure of a thumb, dwells in the middle of the body (in the ether of the heart)." (IV. 12.)

It is elsewhere said to be both infinitely small and infinitely great. The Svetáśvatara Upanishad says:

"The embodied soul is to be thought like the hundredth part of the point of a hair, divided into a hundred parts; he is considered to be infinite." (V. 9.)

The Chhándogya Upanishad says:

"Is the soul within me; it is lighter than a corn, or a barley, or a mustard, or a canary seed, or the substance within it. Such a soul is within me, as is greater than this earth, and greater than the sky, and greater than the heaven, and greater than all these regions [put together]." III. 14, 3.

The Gítá agrees with the Vais'eshika school. Krishna says that the soul is "all-pervading." (II. 24.)

Nehemiah Goreh well remarks, "Those who can believe that the soul of a musquito fills heaven and earth . . . . can believe anything!"

---

[1] *Rational Refutation*, pp. 87, 88.

4. **Is the Soul a part of Brahma or wholly Brahma Itself?**— Several texts seem to intimate that the soul is only a part of Brahma. The Mundaka Upanishad, II. 1, says:

"This is the truth: As its kindred sparks fly out in thousands from a blazing fire, so the various living souls proceed out of that imperishable principle, and return into it again."

The Vedánta-Sútra, II. 3, 43 says:

"(The soul is) a part of the Lord, on account of the declarations of difference, and (because) in a different way also some record that (Brahman) is of the nature of slaves, fishers, and so on."

On the other hand Deussen maintains that "the soul of each one of us is not a part, an emanation of Brahma, but fully and wholly the eternal, indivisible Brahman itself." His reasoning is as follows:

"(1) The soul cannot be different from Brahman, because besides Brahman there is no being; (2) it cannot be regarded as a transformation of Brahman because Brahman is unchangeable; (3) and still less is it a part of Brahman because Brahman has no parts. Nothing remains then but to conclude that the soul is identical with Brahman, that each one of us is the all-unchangeable Brahman, without parts and comprehending in itself all being."[1]

If this is correct, the number of Brahmas must be far beyond computation! Deussen has not the common sense to see the folly into which he is led by his own ratiocinations.

Śankara, in his commentary on the Sútra quoted above, says:

"By 'part' we mean 'a part as it were,' since a being not composed of parts cannot have parts in the literal sense."[2]

Souls, strictly speaking, have no real existence. They are only like the reflection of suns seen in pots of water.

5. **The State of the Soul.**—The condition of the soul during the waking state, dreaming, deep sleep, in a swoon and at death is considered at considerable length by Śankara in his commentaries on the Vedánta-Sútras. Deussen gives the following summary of Vedántic teaching on the subject:

"There are four states of the soul—the waking, the dream, the deep sleep, and death states. In the waking state the soul dwelling in the heart, and in union with the *manas*, consciously rules over the body by the help of the *manas* and *indriyas* (sense-organs). In the dream state the *indriyas* repose, whilst the *manas* remains active; and the soul, encompassed by the *manas* and the *indriyas* which have retreated therein, travels through the veins of the body and then experiences dreams fashioned from the impressions (*vásana*) of the waking state. In the state of deep sleep the union of the soul with the *manas* is dissolved; the *manas* and the *indriyas* now repose, retreating into the veins or pericardium and thence into

[1] *Short Account*, &c. p. 14. [2] Thibaut, Vol. II. 61.

the *mukhyapráṇa* (vital air). The activity of the latter, however, continues, whilst the soul freed from its *upádhis* (limiting adjuncts) enters into Brahman in the ether of the heart. As the soul without the *upádhis* is Brahman itself, this entry into Brahman is only another way of expressing the complete freedom of the soul from the *upádhis*. From this passing absorption into Brahman the soul, on waking, again returns with all its individual characteristics to its previous state."[1]

The Brahma-Sútras say, "In him who is senseless (in a swoon, &c.) there is half union." III. 2. 9.

6. **Condition of Souls at a Mahapralaya.**—Thibaut says:

"At the end of each of the great world periods called Kalpas the Lord (I's'vara) retracts the whole world, *i.e.*, the whole material world is dissolved and merged into non-distinct *Máyá*, while the individual souls, free for the time from actual connection with *upádhis*, lie in deep slumber as it were. But as the consequences of their former deeds are not yet exhausted, they have again to enter on embodied existence as soon as the Lord sends forth a new material world, and the old round of birth, action, death, begins anew to last to all eternity as it lasted from all eternity."[2]

All this is mere imagination, entirely destitute of proof. The Vishnu Purána and other works which describe it contain false geography, false astronomy, &c. Their description of a Mahápralaya is equally untrustworthy.

Remarks on the preceding Statements.

Ignorant Presumption of Hindu Philosophers.—Nehemiah Goreh has the following just remarks on this point:

"The truth is, that the nature of the soul transcends our knowledge, and does not lend itself to description. All that we know of the soul is, that it is something which possesses apprehension, will, and other qualities. More than this we cannot affirm concerning it; as, for instance, that, like earth, water, and other material substances, it has dimension and such like qualities. Much, therefore, that is predicable of a jar, of cloth, and of other material substances, is not to be predicated of the soul. Such, however, is the dispositions of the pandits, that they refuse to consider what things are within the reach of our understanding, and what things lie beyond. They would fain take the visible and the invisible, God and souls included, and measure them, and turn them round and over, and pry into them, and at last get their complete quiddities inside their fist. To their minds, if one is to know anything one should know everything: otherwise, it is better to know nothing. And so they wander on in the wilderness of vain inquiry. I would remind them, that, be the essence of the soul of what sort soever, its origin, duration, and end are in subordination to the will of God; and, therefore if God thinks good that the soul shall exist for ever, it can in no wise incur destruction."[3]

---

[1] *A Short Account, &c.* p. 18. [2] *Vedánta-Sútras*, vol. I. pp. xxvi. xxvii.
[3] *Rational Refutation, &c.* p. 90.

This failing was not peculiar to them. Macaulay says of the philosophers of ancient Europe that "they despised what was practicable, and attempted to solve insoluble enigmas."[1]

Vedantic descriptions of the Human Body, &c., grossly Incorrect.—The Katha Upanishad contains the following:

"16. There are hundred and one arteries of the heart; the one of them (Sushumná,) proceeds to the head. By this (at the time of death) rising upwards (by the door of Áditya) a person gains immortality; or the other (arteries) are of various course." VI. Valli.

The Prasna Upanishad gives the following additional details:

"For the (ether of the) heart is verily that soul. There (arise) the hundred and one (principal) arteries; each of them is a hundred times divided; 72,000 are the branches of every branch artery; within them moves the circulating air." III. 6.

The whole number of arteries is therefore 727,200,000!

The slightest examination of the heart shows that all this is purely imaginary. There are just two branches of a large artery from the heart, containing impure blood, leading to the lungs, and one great artery, which, afterwards, subdivided, conveys pure blood, to the whole body. In like manner, there are two great veins carrying impure blood to the heart from the whole body, and four veins, containing pure blood, leading from the lungs to the heart.

The Prasna Upanishad says that "within the arteries moves the circulating air." *Arteries* mean air-pipes. They were thought to contain only air, because after death they are empty. When a person is alive, blood flows through them. This is proved by the fact that if one of them is cut, blood gushes out. When a person dies, the heart loses its power to send out blood, and the arteries are found empty.

The "three sheaths," "the five vital airs," &c. are similar fictions.

The *Vedánta-Sára* makes the following statement:

"From these gross elements (having the qualities of the five) arise the worlds that are one above the other, *viz.*, *Bhúr*, *Bhuvar*, *Svar*, *Mahar*, *Janas*, *Tapas*, and *Satya*; and those that are beneath the other; called; *Atala*, *Vitala*, *Sutala*, *Rasátala*, *Talátala*, *Mahátala*, *Pátála*; also Brahma's egg (this vaulted world) with the four kinds of gross bodies contained in it, and their food and drink." (See page 35.)

As already mentioned, the Earth is only about 8,000 miles in diameter, and floats in the air, like the moon, moving round the sun. The seven worlds above the earth and the seven below it are all imaginary.

Vedantic Speculation about the Soul as incorrect as those about the Body.—If a traveller gives an account of our own country

[1] *Essay on Bacon.*

which we know to be false, we cannot trust his descriptions of foreign lands. When Vedántists make such mistakes about the *body*, which could easily have been corrected by observation, there is still greater reason to reject their speculations about the *soul*.

Ideas about the soul are chiefly based on the conception of Brahma, described as existing in a state of dreamless repose, unconscious even of its own existence. As each individual soul is asserted to be "fully and wholly the eternal indivisable Brahma itself," it must be of the same character. The soul is said to be like Brahma eternally pure; it neither acts nor enjoys. Practically, like Brahma, it is a non-entity.

As Brahma, according to Vedántism, could do nothing, the fiction of *Máyá* had to be invented to account for the appearance of the universe. As the soul was similarly helpless the figment of an *antaḥ-karaṇa* had to be devised. It is the *antah-karaṇa* which actually cognizes, acts, enjoys, suffers. The soul, amid all its transmigrations, must for ever remain unconscious like Brahma.

As already mentioned, the Vedántic soul is a non-entity, while the *antaḥ-karaṇa* is invested with its functions. The truth is that the Vedántic soul has no existence, while the real soul is the internal ruler. It is the soul which cognizes, acts, does right or wrong, enjoys or suffers either directly or through the body. The soul should be the ruler; the body the servant.

Instead of dogmatizing like Vedántists about the size of the soul, &c., the wisest men confess their ignorance. They believe that they have souls capable of knowing about God, able to distinguish between right and wrong, rendering them responsible beings; but there are insoluble problems connected with them.

Vedantic Arguments for the Eternity of Souls.—One argument for the eternity of the soul is the supposed axiom: "Whatever exists must always have existed." As already shown, this denies God's omnipotence. By His will He can create things or call them out of nothing into existence.

Another argument is that "Whatever had a beginning must have an end." This is also a denial of God's power. He can give a future eternal existence to any creature He has called into being. According to Hinduism, souls may pass into gods, demons, beasts, birds, reptiles, fishes, insects, into plants, and even into inanimate objects. "Who can estimate the number of these eternal *svayambhu* essences! Is it not perfectly unphilosophical, because absolutely unnecessary and egregiously extravagant, to assume such an indefinite number of eternal essences, when one Supreme Essence is sufficient to account for all things, visible or invisible, material or spiritual?"[1]

Vedantism denies the Fatherhood of God.—If our souls are

[1] Dr. K. M. Banerjea, *Dialogues*, p. 164.

eternal and self-existent, we are a sort of miniature gods. Our relation to God is changed. It is only that of king and subjects. His right over us is only that of might. It is only because He is mightier than we and because He possesses power to benefit and to harm us that we should be anxious to pay homage to Him. There is not the love which a child should cherish towards a father. True religion is thus destroyed.

It is a pleasing sign of progress that the Fatherhood of God is beginning to be admitted by educated Hindus. Some even claim that this doctrine is taught in their own sacred books. In the Sástras, Father may be one of the many names given to God; but *not as the source of our existence.* What particularly distinguishes an earthly father is, that under God, he is the author of the child's existence. This can be said of no other person. In that sense neither Brahma nor any Hindu deity can be called father. According to Vedántism and all other systems of Hindu philosophy, souls are as eternal as Brahma himself. The Bible, on the other hand, says, that God is our Father by creation. "Have we not all one Father? Hath not one God created us?" Christianity teaches us to address God as our "Father in heaven." It is true that we have been disobedient, rebellious children, but we are earnestly invited to return, asking forgiveness.

The ancestors of Europeans and Aryan Hindus once worshipped the same God under the same name, *Dyaush-Pitar,* Heaven-Father. Max Müller beautifully says:

> "Thousands of years have passed away since the Aryan nations separated to travel to the North and the South, the West and the East: they have each formed their languages, they have each founded empires and philosophies, they have each built temples and razed them to the ground; they have all grown older, and it may be wiser and better; but when they search for a name for that which is most exalted and yet most dear to every one of us, when they wish to express both awe and love, the infinite and the finite, they can but do what their old fathers did when gazing up to the eternal sky, and feeling the presence of a Being as far as far and as near as near can be; they can but combine the self-same words and utter once more the primeval Aryan prayer, Heaven-Father, in that form which will endure for ever, 'Our Father, which art in heaven.'"[1]

Vedantism denies the Brotherhood of Man.—This is strongly denied by the system of caste, but it is so likewise by the Vedánta. Brothers are children of the same father. As already shown, according to the Vedánta, we have no father, and therefore we are not brothers.

Deussen, with a want of common sense worthy of a Hindu philosopher, tries to improve upon the second commandment of Christianity, "Thou shalt love thy neighbour as thyself." We

[1] *Science of Religion*, pp. 172, 173.

are brothers of the same great Father, and should therefore "love as brethren."

Deussen, in his *Elements of Metaphysics*, thus explains our duty to others:

"You shall love your neighbour as yourselves—because you are your neighbour, and mere illusion makes you believe that your neighbour is something different from yourselves. Or in the words of the Bhagavad Gítá: he, who knows himself in everything and everything in himself, *will not injure himself by himself, na hinasti átmaná átmánam*. This is the sum and tenor of all morality, and this is the standpoint of a man knowing himself as Brahman. He feels himself as *everything*,—so he will not desire anything, for he has whatever can be had; he feels himself *as everything*,—so he will not injure anything, for nobody injures himself." p. 336.

Test this practically. A starving beggar asks charity. The Professor says, "Why do you ask alms of me? You and I are the same; it is mere illusion makes you believe yourself to be different. You will not desire anything, for you have already whatever can be had." Would the beggar be satisfied with such reasoning?[1]

The Christian doctrine is briefly as follows:—

God alone is self-existent, without beginning or end. He is omnipotent, able to call beings or things into existence out of nothing. He gave us a body and a soul. The soul never existed before our present birth. The body is mortal; the soul returns to God who gave it. At the great day of judgment, all must appear before God, to answer for the deeds done in the body, whether good or evil.

As already mentioned, it is unphilosophic to maintain that there are innumerable self-existent beings, when One possessed of almighty power is sufficient. The explanation given by Christianity is beautifully simple, and meets all the requirements of the case.

TRANSMIGRATION.

From the dawn of philosophy, how to account for the suffering in the world has been a great problem. Mansel says:

"Against this immovable barrier of the existence of evil, the waves of philosophy have dashed themselves unceasingly since the birthday of human thought, and have retired broken and powerless, without displacing the minutest fragment of the stubborn rock, without softening one feature of its dark and rugged surface."[2]

Atheism is an attempt to solve the problem. There is so much evil, because there is no Creator or overruling Providence. The great majority of mankind have rejected this theory. How could

[1] See Pice Papers on *The Fatherhood of God* and *The Brotherhood of Man.*

[2] *Limits of Religious Thought.*

a universe so wonderfully constructed have come into existence without an intelligent Creator?

Transmigration is the second attempt to account for the state of the world. It is supposed to be necessary to explain the unequal distribution of happiness and misery which exists. If an infant agonize, it is supposed to arise from a great sin committed in a former birth. On the other hand, if a wicked man prospers, it is thought to be plainly the reward of meritorious actions in a previous state of existence.

The universe is, in Sanskrit, sometimes called *samsára*, denoting motion. It is supposed to consist of innumerable souls and innumerable bodies. The bodies are of all kinds, mineral, vegetable, animal, human, divine, demoniac. Souls are supposed to be constantly leaving their bodies, and seeking other bodies some rising, some falling, others stationary according to their *Karma*. Only in this way, it is imagined, can God be saved from the charge of injustice.

Origin of the Doctrine.—Transmigration is not found in the four Vedas. In them, as already mentioned, a cheerful view is taken of life, and after death a happy reunion with relations is expected in the world of the *Pitris*. The belief arose with Hindu pessimism in the time of the Upanishads, and was intensified by Buddha.

A few quotations may first be given on the subject. The Katha Upanishad says:—

> "7. Some enter the womb (again after death) for assuming a body; others go inside a trunk, according to their works, according to their knowledge." V. Valli.

The Chhándogya Upanishad says:—

> "7. Thereof he, whose conduct is good, quickly attains to some good existence, such as that of a Bráhmana, a Kshatriya or a Vaisya. Next, he who is viciously disposed, soon assumes the form of some inferior creature; such as that of a dog, a hog, or a Chandála." V. 10.

In the Bhagavad Gítá Krishna says to Arjuna:—

> "As a man, having cast off his old garments taketh others that are new, so the embodied (soul) casting off old bodies, entereth others that are new."

The doctrine pervades the whole of the later sacred books of the Hindus, and is universally received. "It is," says Dr. Hooper, "as if every Hindu imbibed it from his mother. With the exception of the few whose thoughts have been changed by Western education, no Hindu seems able to conceive a condition of the universe, which does not involve the truth of this doctrine."[1]

---

[1] *Transmigration*, p. 2.

13

Object to prove that Justice rules the world.—Dr. Hooper says:

"There can be no doubt, that *this* was the original cause of the invention of the theory; as it is still the reason commonly given for maintaining it. Men's instinct of justice is so strong and so uncontrollable, that they cannot be content with the present state of things, in which the good suffer and the wicked enjoy themselves or believe that it can possibly be permanent. And so this system was framed; a system in which the sway of justice is absolute and flawless. According to it, every action must inevitably, sooner or later, receive its exactly due reward, in pleasure or pain. There is no possibility of deviation even by a hair's breadth from strict and infallable justice. The retribution may be long delayed; but come it must with absolute certainty and with undeviating precision."[1]

The doctrine also, as the Rev. T. E. Slater remarks, bear witness to the following truths:

(*a*). To the immortality of the soul; to the continued existence of the soul in a future life.

(*b*). Another important truth witnessed to is the sense of sin, and that sin is inevitably followed by suffering; that demerit must receive its penalty.

(*c*). Further, the soul receives the due reward of its deeds in a body, hereby resembling Christian belief, sharply contrasted with the idea of the ghostly spectres of Greek philosophy.[2]

While the object is good and some great truths are acknowledged, it will be shown, on careful examination, that the doctrine is as untenable as atheism. It makes baseless assumptions, and results in robbing God of His most glorious attribute of mercy.

Objections to the Doctrine.

1. **It is contrary to our Experience.**—By transmigration is meant that the same soul in the course of time takes up its residence in different bodies. Only the *body is changed, the soul is the same soul.* The soul therefore, being the same, possesses the same faculties in its present and in its former births. A traveller who journeys through the earth from city to city carries with him the remembrance of his native place, the persons that he met, and other events that occurred. The soul ought to carry with it a complete remembrance of its past history; but no man has experienced anything of the kind. Any claims to its possession are just as false as those with regard to magical powers.

Dr. Scudder thus answers an objection:—

"It will not do to say that you have forgotten those things just as you have forgotten things which occurred in your infancy. It is quite true that you cannot remember matters which took place during your

---

[1] *Transmigration*, pp. 4, 5. [2] *Christian College Magazine*, Vol. xv. p. 262.

infancy in this present birth. It would not be strange, therefore, that you should fail to recall what happened during your infancy in a former birth. But if you really existed in a former birth, you surely were not infants throughout its entire duration. Did you not then grow into youth? Did you not attain to manhood? Did you not marry? Did you not work hard for a living? Did you not toil for the support of your children? Did you not feel hunger and thirst, disease and pain? Did you not experience joys and sorrows innumerable? Can it be possible that you have entirely forgotten all this? Surely the thoughts and words and deeds of a previous existence could not all have thus passed into entire forgetfulness! Know clearly that you never existed before the present birth."[1]

It is objected that we cannot recall the events of our former births, because we are under the power of *máyá*, or illusion. How is it that *máyá* extends only to alleged former births and not to the present? The fact is that one false theory is attempted to be supported by another. We cannot recollect events in alleged former births, because they had no existence. We remember the present life, *máyá* notwithstanding, because we have really existed.

2. **It fails to explain the Origin of things.**—Deussen says:

"No life can be the first, for it is the fruit of previous actions, nor the last, for its actions must be expiated in a next following life."[2]

The advocates of the doctrine have been forced to deny that the universe ever had a beginning. Inequalities in life are said to be the results of peculiar habits and works in a previous state of existence. This only removes the difficulty one single step, for the question will recur, *Whence those peculiar habits and works?*—and, whence the inequalities *in that life?* Thus Hindus were compelled to fly from stage to stage, until they were forced to declare that the world was never created—that it is without beginning, that it is eternal. And that which is eternal is, in their conception, not dependent on a cause. How can such men consistently find fault with the Chárvákas, who deny the necessity of an intelligent First Cause, when they themselves pronounce the world to be without a beginning? The theory involves difficulties far greater than those it is intended to remove.

Before there could be merit or demerit, beings must have existed and acted. The first in order could no more have been produced by *Karma* than a hen could be born from her own egg. Sankarácharya ridicules the idea of an eternal succession of works and creations as a troop of blind leaders of the blind. However far back we go, the same impossibility remains.

3. **It is Unjust.**—The object of transmigration is to purify the soul by lessons of warning from past history. This is lost when a person knows not what he did and why he is punished. Suppose a magistrate said to a peon, "Give that man fifty lashes," would

---

[1] *Bazar Addresses.* [2] *Elements of Metaphysics*, p. 329.

the man not ask, "Why am I flogged?" What would be thought of such a magistrate? What is the use of shutting up a soul in the body of a pig, which has no sense of degradation, which cannot possibly know either that it has ever committed a fault or that it is suffering the penalty due to that fault? It is said that if a man has stolen paddy he will be born a rat, whose chief occupation is to steal paddy. A man must, by way of atoning for one act of theft, become a thief all his life![1]

Should a son be hanged because his father committed murder? According to transmigration, people suffer, not on account of their own deeds; but, as it were, for those of their ancestors of which they know nothing.

For if a man is so changed at each birth as to forget all his previous history, he becomes virtually a new being. What he suffers now he suffers on account of sins committed by another; and these sufferings he has no choice but to endure. Even the very sins a man now commits are punishments of previous sins, and he cannot but commit them. Their punishment, again, he cannot bear in this life if he would; they must be borne by him in another birth, when the loss of all consciousness of the present has made him, in fact, another person. His present happiness is the reward of a previous person's good deeds, his present good deeds will be rewarded to some future person. In all this there is an absence of justice.[2]

4. **It denies Divine Mercy.**—The Rev. Dr. Hooper has the following remarks on this point:—

"The system of Transmigration leaves absolutely no room for divine mercy. Four of the six philosophical systems do, indeed, acknowledge an 'I'śwara'; but what for? His *one* work is to arrange that each soul shall enjoy or suffer precisely the fruit of his doings, shall enter the body which exactly suits his deserts. In other words, I'śwara's one work is to carry out strict, unswerving *justice*. *He has nothing whatever to do with mercy.* There is no possible room for it in the system. The very slightest exercise of mercy would be, so far, a derogation from the completeness of the system of Transmigration, a blot on its fair name. What then? Do not Hindus believe in divine mercy? Indeed they do; and that in two ways, but both are entirely irrespective of, indeed they ignore, Transmigration. The statement, "I's'wara dayálu hai" (God is merciful) is one which very few Hindus indeed would not subscribe to. So far have foreign influences permeated the modern Hindu mind, that very few indeed perceive, what however is obvious to any one who thinks, that the above statement is a flat contradiction, so far as it extends, of the Doctrine of Transmigration."

Hindus accept the most contradictory doctrines. *Sankaráchárya* says that even I'śvara cannot alter *Karma* any more than he can produce rice out of wheat seed. Yet it is believed that all

[1] From Dr. Scudder.

[2] Abridged from Robson's *Hinduism and Christianity*, 2nd Ed. pp. 191, 192.

sins may be washed away by bathing in the Ganges or other supposed sacred waters.

The *Epiphany* thus strikingly shows the cruelty of the supposed system of transmigration and the helplessness of God:

"In reality, the suggested solution only seems to lead us into greater difficulties than ever. God did not create souls, or affix their varying characters or *karmas*; they have existed thus eternally, in independence of Him. Granted this, the question at once arises, who or what is responsible for these cruel variations and inequalities? These eternally existing souls suffer from a strange injustice, also existing from eternity, and apparently they will eternally so suffer. Partiality is then coeval, and coeternal with finite existence; is inherent in the very nature of things. Who or what is the author of this harsh and arbitrary law of *karma* that has thus been going on and will thus go on for ever?"

"The system only seems to make the injustice of the universe more irremediable and more hopeless: it is eternal, necessary, and cannot be bettered. God himself can only look on eternally at the course of things as a helpless spectator, compelled by some cruel necessity to apportion reward and punishment, according to an unjust law over which He has no control; He cannot intervene to re-adjust the harsh measure that has been meted out by a power independent of Him, or redress the eternally wrong balance. Human life is beyond His control altogether: He is conniving, from sheer impotence, at a great scheme of eternal injustice." December 13, 1895.

Christianity, on the other hand, shows how Divine Justice and Mercy are reconciled through Jesus Christ.

5. **It leads people to impute the results of their own misconduct in this life to sins in a former birth.**—The chief sufferings of men are caused by poverty, sickness, and evil conduct. Poverty is often occasioned by laziness or want of thrift. One great reason why the people of India are poor is their extravagant expenditure on marriages. Most sickness is caused by bad water, filth, and unwholesome food. When people believe that their misfortunes arise from sins in a former birth, they rest contented and make no efforts to remove them.

A father neglects his child and allows him to mix with bad companions. He turns out a drunkard, gambler, and thief. The father, instead of blaming himself, attributes the misconduct of his sons to sins in a former birth. The constant excuse for almost everything that ought not to be is, "What can we do? It is all the fruit of former births." Even murderers comfort themselves with such an excuse.

Deussen says that the doctrine is "a consolation in the distresses of life." *The Hindu* forms a different estimate of its effects. "The contentment of our people is the result of moral death during centuries." The tendency is to lead people to submit to evils instead of trying to remedy them.

5. **It discourages Virtue and encourages Vice.**—The effects of rewards and punishments depend greatly upon their nearness. If very far off, they have very little influence. According to transmigration, people here eat the fruit, sweet or bitter, of actions in former births, while good or evil deeds in this life will be rewarded or punished in some future birth, how distant no one can tell. The natural tendency is therefore what is described.

The Christian doctrine is that we never existed before our present life. This is confirmed by universal human experience. We are here in a state of probation, and shall be rewarded or punished after death, and shall not transmigrate.

A few other observations may be offered.

1. **Inequalities of happiness are less than is supposed.**—There are many poor men far happier than the rich. There is a proverb: "The fruit of austerities, a kingdom; the fruit of a kingdom, hell." Great men are tempted to vices from which the poor are free. Wealth and power are, not unfrequently, a curse rather than a blessing.

2. **We can look forward as well as backward.**—The *Epiphany* says:

> "It seems possible to interpret the puzzling inequalities of life at least as well on the theory of *probation* as on the theory of *retribution*. And to effect this, different kinds of moral development are necessary. One soul is developed to perfection through the process of adversity, another through that of prosperity. The former may be the higher mode; but both courses have their appropriate tests and crises for free will to go through. We believe that all inequalities will be redressed and exhibited in their true light at the Last Judgment, when it will be seen that "many who are first shall be last.' The justice of God will then be manifest, and till that time we can wait in faith."

3. **Most of our sufferings are caused by our breach of God's righteous law and are intended for our amendment.**

God has made us *persons*, and not *things*. We are not like watches which can only act as they are moved. We have the power of *self-determination*, we are free to do wrong if we choose. But things are so ordered that, as a rule, sin, in the end, leads to suffering. The burning words of Kingsley ought to be impressed upon the minds of all:

> "Foremost among them stands a law which I must insist on, boldly and perpetually, a law which man has been trying in all ages, as now, to deny, or at least to ignore; though he might have seen it, if he had willed, working steadily in all times and nations, And that is—that as the fruit of righteousness is wealth and peace, strength and honour; the fruit of unrighteousness is poverty and anarchy, weakness and shame. It is an ancient doctrine and yet one ever young."[1]

---

[1] *Limits of Exact Science applied to History.*

The Rev. T. E. Slater says:

"Happiness and misery are very largely the result of our own character and conduct here and now. The idle, the imprudent, the intemperate, live in poverty and suffering; while the industrious and the virtuous, as a rule, enjoy prosperity and happiness.

"The conditions of life depend, too, very much on the *conduct of others.* If a man does good, others will be benefited; if evil, others will suffer. Why do so many suffer? Not because they are in fault; not because God is partial; but because they happened to live near one another. If all men were good and honest and just in their dealings with others, there would be far less misery in the world. By removing the evils that men inflict on one another, one reason assigned for the belief in transmigration would disappear."[1]

4. **Children inherit largely the Characteristics of their Parents.**—This is called the doctrine of 'heredity,' a demonstrated proof, instead of a mere assumption, like transmigration, invented in an age ignorant of modern science.

"Not our own virtues and vices contracted in some former birth, but the virtues and vices of those who have lived before us reach into our time; and moral and intellectual qualities, virtues and vicious habits, and certain diseases, are all in the stream of heritage which flows from the distant past."[2]

This shows how careful parents ought to be. Their conduct affects, not only themselves, but their posterity. They may leave them a heritage of blessing or woe.

5. **We are much influenced by our Surroundings.**—This is called the law of 'environment.' A child born among vicious people is almost certain to follow their example; while one brought up among the virtuous may be hoped to imitate them. Reformatories have been established by some Christian Governments by which young criminals have frequently been led to lead new lives.

6. **Affliction, properly improved, may have a most beneficial influence on the character.**—

A holy man of old said, "It is good for me that I have been afflicted. Before I was afflicted I went astray; but now have I kept Thy word." Millions upon millions have had the same experience. Good men, who suffer affliction rightly, come out of it purified, like gold which has been tried by fire. Many parents have been led by the sickness and death of their children to think of a world where there is no more pain or death, and where they shall meet again their loved ones, never more to be separated.

"Life," says Dr. Fairbairn, "is all the nobler from being a battle against evil; all the worthier to be lived that its Maker has designed that it should at once educate and redeem through suffering."[3]

---

[1] *Christian College Magazine*, Vol. XV. p. 271.
[2] Rev. T. E. Slater, *Christian College Magazine*, Vol. XV. p. 273.
[3] *The City of God*, p. 186.

7. **"I know not, God knoweth."**—It is admitted that, after all the explanations which can be offered, there is a residue which is inexplicable. We are like young children trying to understand the government of a mighty empire.

"What am I?
An infant crying in the night;
An infant crying for the light;
And with no language but a cry."

"Behind the veil, behind the veil," in a future state of existence, then God's ways to man will be justified. "What I do thou knowest not now, but thou shalt know hereafter." Meanwhile

"Falling with my weight of cares,
Upon the great world's altar stairs
That slope thro' darkness up to God,
I stretch lame hands of faith and grope.

Oh yet we trust that somehow good
Will be the final goal of ill."

At all events, the above explanation is far better than atheism, transmigration, or any other which has been offered. A belief in the doctrine of transmigration is now confined to uncivilised or half-civilised nations.

Some of the injurious effects of the belief in the doctrine upon Hindus are thus stated by Mr. Slater:

"The transmigration of the soul has always been regarded as the direst calamity by people of India—as the root of all evil. The soul is tossed hither and thither, at the mercy of a force set in motion by itself alone, but which can never be arrested, because its operation depends on past actions wholly beyond control and even unremembered. Hence the desire of means to put a stop to further transmigration, to shorten the duration of the wanderings, has been the object of philosophical research in all the systems.

"And is not this one great reason why the Hindu has declined in power and degenerated? He feels held as by an iron hand in the dread bonds of fate, from which even death allows no escape, but only sets him revolving in an endless cycle of being; whereas his younger brother of the West, under the bracing influence of a more joyous faith, knowing himself to be a son of God, and possessing in Christ a blessed immortality, has widened with the 'process of the suns.' There is little doubt which is the more acceptable and invigorating creed."[1]

"The system has now been going on for thousands of years; has the Hindu nation become better, age after age? Its own shastras say, No. The *first* age was the age of truth—the *Krita* age: the present is the *Kali Yuga,* the age of ignorance, folly, and sin; one 'period' of which is now drawing to a close. Is it not the universal lamentation of Hindu reformers that the nation has degenerated? And any improvement that is taking place at the present time, is due, not to the belief in transmigration, but to foreign influences that are, indirectly, destructive of it."[2]

---

[1] *Christian College Magazine,* Vol. XV. p. 279. [2] *Ibid,* p. 337.

THE GREAT SENTENCES.

TAT TWAM ASI, 'That thou art.'
BRAHMASMI, 'I am Brahma.'

The assertions are that Brahma and the Soul are identical; that the soul may say, "I am Brahma."

With regard to the first text, Gough remarks:

"In the view of the Indian schoolmen, the greatest of all the texts of the Upanishads is the text, That art thou, in the sixth Lecture of the Chhāndogya Upanishad. This is pre-eminently the Mahāvākya, the supreme announcement. It is on the comprehension of this text that spiritual intuition (*samyagdarśana*) or ecstatic vision rises in the purified intelligence of the aspirant to extrication from metempsychosis" (*samsára*).

"The sense is this: the individual soul is one with the universal Soul, and the universal Soul is one with the one and only Self."[1]

The Prabuddha Bhárata says:

Vedánta "is the one philosophy which dares to call man God Himself, not merely the son of God or His servant." Vol. I. p. 75.

The Brahmavádin (Oct. 12, 1895, p. 30) makes the same claim in terms equally blasphemous:

"Man is not the mere creature of a God; he is God himself. He has not simply the image impressed upon him of his Creator. He is himself the Creator."

The two main proofs in the *Vedánta-Sára* are the following:

I. There is no difference between things taken collectively and distributively, as there is none between a forest and its trees, or between a lake and its waters. Page 30.

This is supposed to prove that there is no difference between Brahma and an individual soul.

It is true that there is no difference between a forest and *all* the trees taken together; but an *individual* tree cannot say "I am the *forest*."

In like manner a house is equal to all the bricks of which it is composed, but a single *brick* cannot say "I am the *house*." A lakh of rupees is equal to a hundred thousand rupees, but a rupee is not therefore equal to a lakh.

In logic this reasoning is called the Fallacy of Division. It consists in arguing from the collective to the distributive use of a term.

II. The second great argument is founded on the sentence, "This is that same Devadatta."

Hence, This = that; Twam = Tat.

It is asserted that Tat and Twam "refer to one and the same

[1] *Philosophy of the Upanishads*, pp. 89, 94.

thing"; that they are "related as subject and predicate"; as "indicator and indicated." pp. 40, 41.

The sentence, "This is that same Devadattá," is what is called in logic a *petitio principii*, a begging of the principle in question, taking a thing for true and drawing conclusions from it as such, when it requires to be proved before any conclusions can be deduced from it.

It is true that differences in point of time and other non-essentials are acknowledged; but it is held that they agree substantially. This is attempted to be proved by a subtle chain of false reasoning, pp. 42-44. After comparing the attributes of *Tat* and *Twam*, let it be decided whether they are the same.

Tat, God.	*Twam*, Man.
The Creator	A Creature.
Eternal	Began to be.
Omnipresent	Confined to a small space.
Omniscient	Parviscient.
Omnipotent	Parvipotent.
Unchangeable	Subject to change.
Infinitely Holy	Sinful.
Infinitely Happy	Subject to misery.

If two beings with attributes so different are the same, so are light and darkness, knowledge and ignorance, virtue and vice:

Gauḍapúrṇánanda thus contrasts the two:

"Thou art verily rifled, O thou animal soul, of thy understanding, by this dark theory of Máyá, because like a maniac, thou constantly ravest, 'I am Brahma.' Where is thy divinity, thy sovereignty, thy omniscience? Ou thou animal soul! thou art as different from Brahma as is a mustard seed from Mount Meru. Thou art a finite soul, He is infinite. Thou canst occupy but one space at a time, He is always everywhere. Thou art momentarily happy or miserable, He is happy at all times. How canst thou say 'I am He?' Hast thou no shame?"[1]

Rámánujà, another celebrated Hindu writer, argues against it similarly:

"The word *tat* (it) stands for the ocean of immortality, full of supreme felicity. The word *twam* (thou) stands for a miserable person, distracted through fear of the world. The two cannot therefore be one. They are substantially different. He is to be worshipped by the whole world. Thou art but His slave. How could there be an image or reflection of the infinite and spotless One? There may be a reflection of a finite substance; how could there be such a thing of the Infinite? How canst thou, oh slow of thought! say, I am He, who has set up this immense sphere of the universe in its fulness? By the mercy of the most High a little understanding has been committed to thee; it is not for thee, oh perverse one, to say, therefore I am God."[2]

[1] Banerjea's *Dialogues*, p. 378. [2] *Ibid*, p. 408.

Taking the words in their plain meaning, the climax of Hindu philosophy is a blasphemous falsehood, too horrible almost to be mentioned. With Satanic pride, a puny, ignorant, sinful, mortal presumes to say, "I am God!" When he believes this monstrous lie, according to Hindu philosophy, he is the only wise man! How true are the words, "Professing themselves to be wise, they became fools."

MUKTI OR LIBERATION.

Grand Aim of Hindu Philosophy.—As already mentioned, Hindu philosophy arose when a pessimistic view began to be taken of life—when existence was regarded as a curse, and freedom from future births was considered the highest good. All the six systems agree in this. Gough says:

> "This philosophy was a new religion, with a new promise, a religion, not of the many, but of the few. The promise is no longer a promise of felicity in this life or in a higher life, but a promise of release from the sorrows of the heart, of a repose unbroken by a dream, of everlasting peace, in which the soul shall cease to be a soul, and shall be merged in the one and only Self the characterless being, characterless thought, and characterless beatitude."[1]

This freedom from future births is called *mukti* or *moksha*, liberation. The doctrine is not found in the four Vedas; it is a later development.

Means to be employed.—Mukti is supposed to be attained when a person realizes the great sentence, *Brahmásmi.*

There are two main stages—meditation *with* an object and meditation *without* an object. The means to be employed for both are described at length in pp. 46—49 of the Vedánta-Sára translation, and more fully in the *Yoga Sútras* of Patanjali.

The object is to attain likeness to Brahma, represented as in a state of dreamless sleep.

Yama ('Forbearance'), and *niyama*, 'Religious Observances,' are both enjoined as subservient to the object in view. As explained in the Vedánta-Sára, Acts of 'Forbearance' are not killing, not lying, not stealing, chastity, and not accepting gifts. 'Religious Observances' are purifications, contentment, penance, study, and persevering meditations on I'svara."

But other special means are necessary.

Patanjali defines *yoga* as follows:

> "*Yoga* is the suppression of the transformations of the thinking principle." I. 2.[2]

---

[1] *Philosophy of the Upanishads* p. 262.

[2] Translation by Manilal Nabhubhai Dvivedi, p. 1.

According to Hindu philosophy, the mind assumes the form of any object seen or conceived. The number of such changes daily must be almost countless. The design of Yoga is to put a stop to the transformations of the mind, so that at last meditation may be objectless.

Mechanical means were also employed.

Asana.—There were various modes of disposing the hands, feet, &c., one or two of which may be described.

The Lotus Posture.—The right foot should be placed on the left thigh, and the left foot on the right thigh; the hands should be crossed, and the two great toes should be firmly held thereby; the chin should be bent down to the chest; and in this posture the eyes should be directed to the tip of the nose.

Gomukha, or Cow's Mouth Posture.—Put the right ankle on the left side of the chest, and similarly the left ankle on the right side.

Fowl Posture.—Having established the lotus posture, if the hand be passed between the thigh and the knees and placed on the earth so as to lift the body aloft, it will produce the fowl seat.

Pranayama, the regulation of the breath, is also considered of great importance. It is thus described:

> "The usual mode is after assuming the posture prescribed, to place the ring finger of the right hand on the left nostril, pressing it so as to close it, and to expire with the right, then to press the right nostril with the thumb, and to inspire through the left nostril, and then to close the two nostrils with the ring finger and the thumb, and to stop all breathing. The order is reversed in the next operation, and in the third act the first form is required."[1]

Other exercises are mentioned:

> "*Uḍḍiyána* consists in drawing in the navel and the parts above and below it. *Múlabandha* consists in drawing in the parts of the anus, and in mentally exerting as if to draw the *apána* upward towards the navel. The *jálandhara* consists in pressing the chin to the heart." III. 58, 27. Appendix v.

Marvellous powers are attributed to the man fully initiated in the Yoga. The past and present are unveiled to his gaze. He sees things invisible to others. He hears the sounds that are in distant worlds. He becomes stronger than the elephant, bolder than the lion, swifter than the wind. He mounts at pleasure into the air or dives into the depths of the earth and the ocean. He acquires mastery over all things, whether animated or inanimate.

The whole belief is a delusion. The brain is the organ of the mind. To enable it to act properly, it must have a good supply of pure blood. The blood is purified by fresh air entering into the

[1] Quoted by Mr. R. C. Bose from the translation of the Yoga Shastra by Dr. Rajendralála Mitra.

lungs by breathing. From want of sufficient food and suppression of the breath, the blood of the Yogi is small in quantity and impure. The brain does not act properly. He may be in a dreamy condition or almost unconscious. Barth, a French writer, a distinguished Orientalist, says of Yoga exercises:

"Conscientiously observed they can only issue in folly and idiocy."[1]

Jivanmukta.—The last section into which the *Vedánta-Sára* has been divided treats of the *Jívanmukta*, 'liberated but still living.'

Colonel Jacob says:

"According to the Systems, works are of three kinds, viz., accumulated (*sanchita*), fructescent (*prárabdha*), and current (*kriyamána*). The first are the works of former births which have not yet borne fruit; the second are those which have brought about the present life, and so have begun to bear fruit; and the third are those which are being performed during the present life, and which will bear fruit in a future one. According to the Vedánta, the true knowledge of Brahma and of one's own identity with It burns up the accumulated works and cancels the effects of the current ones. The fruits of the fructescent ones must be exhausted during the present life, and then at death emancipation is realised."[2]

The Jívanmukta is experiencing these fructescent fruits, which cannot be destroyed by the knowledge of Brahma. "But, according to the Yoga, the meditation which is styled in that system *asamprajnáta*, 'meditation without an object,' *can* destroy them, and so is considered by Yogins to be superior to knowledge."[3]

Deussen gives the following account of the *Jívanmukta*:

"42. *Abolition of all Duties.*—As for the wise man, there is no world, no body, no further sufferings, there is also for him no further obligation to action. For all that he will do no evil, for false illusion, the cause of all action good or bad, has been annihilated. Whether he performs any more works or not is a matter of indifference, whether he does them or not, they are not his works and do not cling to him. It is difficult to say if rules of conduct, expressing themselves in justice and love, are necessary for the wise man who has acquired the knowledge that he himself is Brahma. Such rules may be found in the *Bhagavad Gítá*, but not in the writings of Sankara."[4]

Jívanmuktas are said to be subject to no law; to them there is no such thing as virtue and vice. In support of this Col. Jacob quotes the following:

"By no deed soever is his future bliss harmed, not by theft, not by a

---

[1] *Religions of India.* p. 83.

[2] *Hindu Pantheism*, p. 125.

[3] A full account of Yoga exercises, with the wonderful powers they are alleged to confer, is given in YOGA SASTRA: the Yoga Sútras of Patanjali Examined, 8vo. 78 pp. 2½ As. Post-free 3 As. Sold by Mr. A. T. Scott, Tract Depôt, Madras.

[4] *Short Account of the Vedanta Philosophy*, p. 24.

Bráhman's murder, nor by a mother's murder, nor by a father's murder; nor, if he wishes to commit sin, departs the bloom from his face."

Kaushítaki-Upanishad, iii. 1. (Cowell.)

"The thought afflicts him not, 'What good have I left undone, what evil done?'"

Taittiríya-Upanishad, ii. 9. (Gough.)

"He is not defiled by an evil deed."

Brihadáranyaka, 4, 4, 23.[1]

It is argued, however, that such passages in the Sruti and Smriti are merely designed to extol the position of the enlightened man, and not to impel him to act in the manner there described."[2]

Final Liberation.—Deussen says:

"After works, whereof the fruit has not yet appeared, have been annihilated by knowledge, and those, whereof the fruit pertains to this present existence have come to their term with the completion of the present life, full and eternal release comes to the knower at the moment of death; the spirits of his life do not depart, but he is Brahman and into Brahman is he absorbed. 'As streams flow and vanish in the ocean, losing name and form, so does the wise soul, resigning name and form, pass into the heavenly and supreme Spirit.'"[3]

The condition of the liberated soul must be similar to that of Brahma itself. As already explained, it is compared to a state of dreamless sleep, in which the sleeper is unconscious of his own existence, and happy only in the sense of being free from the miseries of *Samsára.* Virtually the happiness is that of a stone. Wilson says:

"Annihilation, then, as regards individuals, is as much the ultimate destiny of the soul as it is of the body, and '*Not to be*' is the melancholy result of the religion and philosophy of the Hindus."[4]

Liberation merely the End of a Dream.—Gough quotes the following:

"On the liberation of the sage, to use the language of the *Viveka-chúdámani,* all things visible melt away into the original Self, as the darkness faints and melts away before the rising sun. Its fictitiously limiting mind with all its modes has been dissolved, and the soul is the Self again; the jar is broken, and the ether that was in it is one with the one and undivided ether, from which the jar once seemed to sever it. The sage has seen the Self, and passed into oneness with it, lost like a water-drop in water. His implication in metempsychosis, and his extrication from it, have been but figments of the cosmic fiction; unreal as the snake that appears and vanishes in place of the piece of rope, to the eyes of the belated traveller. He has had life after life from time without beginning, but these were but a series of dreams. At last he is awake, and his dream-lives are nullities. In pure verity it is only the Self that ever is or has been. The world has neither come into being nor passed

---

[1] *Hindu Pantheism,* p. 128. Other similar quotations are made.
[2] *Ibid,* p. 129. [3] *A Short Account of the Vedánta Philosophy,* p. 24.
[4] *Essays on the Religion of the Hindus,* ii. 114. Quoted by Col. Jacob.

out of being. There has been no fatal migration of the soul, no worshipper seeking recompense or mental purity, no sage yearning after liberation, and no soul has been liberated. These things were phantasmagoric figments, a play of semblances, a darkness, an absence of light. Now the light is veiled no more, and remains a pure undifferenced light, and is in truth the only thing that ever has been and ever is."[1]

Remarks on Mukti.

1. **The Aim is purely Selfish.**—There is neither thought nor effort for others; the attention of the Vedántist is concentrated upon himself. In this he is simply imitating Brahma, according to the proverb, "As is the god, so is the worshipper."

2. **There is no desire to become wiser and more useful; no aspirations for deliverance from the burden of sin and for a purer and higher character: there is only a yearning for release from the miseries of life.**

Gough says:

"The Indian sages, as the Upanishads picture them, seek for participation in the divine life, not by pure feeling, high thought, and strenuous endeavour—not by an unceasing effort to learn the true and do the right,—but by the crushing out of every feeling and every thought, by vacuity, apathy, inertion, and ecstasy. They do not for a moment mean that the purely individual feelings and volitions are to be suppressed in order that the philosopher may live in free obedience to the monitions of a higher common nature. Their highest Self (Brahma) is little more than an empty name. Their pursuit is not a pursuit of perfect character, but of perfect characterlessness. They place perfection in the pure indetermination of thought, the final residence of prolonged abstraction; not in the higher and higher types of life and thought successively intimated in the idealising tendencies of the mind, as among the progressive portions of the human race."[2]

3. **The Happiness is only that of a Stone.**—To exist for ever in a state of dreamless sleep, unconscious of existence, is only the happiness of an inanimate object.

Vedántism is well summed up by Mr. Ram Chandra Bose in the following words:

"*It begins with a recognition of human sorrow, goes out in vain quest of a proper remedy, and ultimately arrives at annihilation as the goal where human misery terminates only with the extinction of life.*"[3]

The Christian View of Heaven.—The Christian conception of God is very different from that of the Vedántic Brahma. As already explained, He is never unconscious of His own existence;

---

[1] *Philosophy of the Upanishads*, pp. 60, 61

[2] *Ibid*, pp. 266, 267.

[3] *Hindu Philosophy*, p. 363.

He never slumbers nor sleeps. He knows whatever happens throughout His vast dominions, and His ear is ever open to the cry of His children. He is the fountain of life, wisdom, holiness, and bliss. In heaven His creatures behold Him in unclouded splendour, and are filled with joy unspeakable and full of glory. They are continually growing in wisdom and holiness, and, we may believe, becoming greater and greater blessings to all around them. The special happiness of heaven is that it is *eternal*. There is no passing from heaven to hell as according to Hinduism. Those who enter there shall be "for ever with the Lord." The Christian does not get to heaven by his own merit, but as a gift of God, and hence he has no fear of his merit being exhausted, and that he will have to fall down again to this world of sin and sorrow.

The Rev. Nehemiah Goreh thus contrasts his feelings as a Christian and a Hindu with regard to his duty to God :—

"Since Christianity has taught me that God gave me my very being, I have begun to acknowledge that my obligation of worshipping, honouring and loving Him would not cease as long as I had my being. So our Scriptures also expressly teach us. The holy Psalmist says: 'Praise the Lord, O my soul. While I live I will praise the Lord. I will sing praises unto my God *while I have any being*.' I, as a Christian, have been taught to believe that to love and glorify God is the very end of my existence. In this will consist my eternal joy and happiness. Not so was my faith when I was a Hindu. The state of salvation, according to my belief at that time, was to be free from transmigration, and to be separated, not only from the body, but even from the *antah-karana*, which is the organ of all our thoughts and consciousness, and to remain unconscious for ever. Indeed the teaching of the Vedánta, which represents the orthodox view, and which I followed, is that souls, when saved, became Brahma itself, and of course lose their individual consciousness. So then, according to teaching of the Vedánta as well as according to all other ancient schools of religion among the Hindus, worship of God is only possible until one obtains salvation."

EUROPEAN ESTIMATES OF THE VEDANTA.

Of late much importánce has been attached to the favourable opinions of the Vedánta expressed by Schopenhauer and Max Müller. They may be briefly noticed. The former says:

"In the whole world there is no study so beneficial and so elevating as that of the Oupnek'hat. It has been the solace of my life, it will be the solace of my death."

Schopenhauer's knowledge of what he called the 'Oupnek'-hat' (Upanishads) was derived from a Latin translation, made by a Frenchman from a Persian translation. The Latin translation Max Müller admits was written "in an utterly unintelligible style."

Schopenhauer has been called the "Founder of Modern Pessimism"—that everything in nature is the worst, that life is essentially an evil, and the duty of man is to seek extinction of being. This is Hinduism. Its grand enquiry is not, what is truth? but, how to cut short the 84 lakhs of births?

Schopenhauer defined himself as a "despiser of men:"

> "In woman he saw only a wayward, mindless animal—ugly too, he said—existing solely for the propagation of the species, an end which perpetuated the woe of the world."[1]

Schopenhauer claimed that the study of the Upanishads was "beneficial and elevating." It certainly failed to produce that effect on himself. His character is thus described: "His disposition was heavy and severe, dark, mistrustful and suspicious, preventing him from entering into permanent trustful relations with men or women."[2] After the death of his father, he treated his mother with such insolence, that she could not live in the same house with him.

Max Müller adds that Schopenhauer was "certainly not a man given to deal in extravagant praise of any philosophy but his own." This is quite true, but his "extravagant praise" of the Upanishads arose from the fact that he thought he was praising "his own philosophy."

Max Müller, after quoting the opinion of Schopenhauer, adds:

> "If these words of Schopenhauer's required any endorsement, I should willingly give it as the result of my own experience during a long life devoted to the study of many philosophies and many religions.
>
> "If philosophy is meant to be a preparation for a happy death, or euthanasia, I know of no better preparation for it than the Vedánta philosophy."[3]

The *Brahmavádin* quotes the following as from Max Müller:

> "As it has been well remarked by no less an authority than Max Müller, her Vedanta, while being the most sublime philosophy, is also the most satisfying religion." Sept. 14, 1895.

Professor Max Müller is just the opposite, in some respects, of Schopenhauer. He

> "loveth well
> Both man and bird, and beast."

In his intercourse with every one he seeks to be as pleasant as possible. It should, however, be remembered that he has "Two Voices." By listening only to one of them, a very erroneous conclusion may be drawn. The Professor's proviso must also be taken into account. Writing to the *Brahmavádin* he says:

---

[1] *Upanishads*, vol. I., p. lviii.
[2] Chambers' *Encyclopædia*, vol. ix., p. 221.
[3] *Lectures on the Vedánta Philosophy*, p. 8.

"I spend my happiest hours in reading Vedantic books. They are to me like the light of the morning, like the pure air of the mountains—so simple, so true, if once understood." Dec. 7, 1897.

Observe the qualification, "if once understood." The fact is that the Professor, like Schopenhauer, has his private interpretation of Vedántism. He and S'ankara differ on some important points.

Colonel Jacob resided in India for 29 years, and made Hindu Philosophy his speciality. He has published several works on Vedánta[1] and compiled a Concordance to the *Upanishads*. Max Müller's *Lectures on the Vedánta Philosophy* were reviewed by Colonel Jacob in *The Academy*. While giving them credit for presenting the system in "an extremely lucid and attractive form," it is claimed that the author apparently does not clearly understand one of its leading features:

"The great philosopher S'ankara gives clear definitions of God and Brahman, but, not infrequently, as I have shown in my recent edition of the text of the *Vedánta-sára*, he ignores the distinction between them, although that distinction is one of the main features of his system. Amongst us, at any rate, to avoid confusion, the term Brahman (neuter) should be strictly confined to the pure, unassociated, Brahman; whilst God is Brahma-associated-with ignorance. In the work before us Prof. Max Müller has not preserved this distinction with sufficient care. We read:

'The Self can never be known as objective, but can only be itself, and thus be conscious of itself.... it knows, but it cannot be known' (p. 67). 'Whose very being is knowing, and whose knowing is being' (p. 70). 'The only attributes of this Brahman, if attributes they can be called, are that he is, that he knows, and that he is full of bliss' (p. 71). 'The soul or Self has but three qualities. It is, it perceives, and it rejoices' (p. 94). 'Brahman was before the creation of the world, and had always something to know and think upon' (p. 139).

"Now a Vedantist of S'ankara's schools would take exception to every one of these statements, and rightly so; for to attribute to pure Brahman perception, knowing, thinking, rejoicing, or even consciousness, is to destroy his system of non-duality."

In defence of Max Müller it may be said that the Upanishads, which are full of contradictions, in some passages assert that Brahma *knows*; but the true doctrine of Vedánta on the subject is as stated above.

The Professor also seems to regard as blasphemous another doctrine of S'ankara—the *identity* of Brahman and the individual Self or Soul.[2]

The Professor's "Second Voice" may now be quoted. He says in his *Lectures on the Vedánta Philosophy*:

"I know I have often been blamed for calling rubbish what to the Indian mind seemed to contain profound wisdom, and to deserve the

[1] *For list of them, see Prefatory Note.* [2] *Lectures*, p. 107.

highest respect .... Every attempt to discover reason in what is unreasonable is accepted as legitimate so long as it enables us to keep what we are unwilling to part with. Still it cannot be denied that the Sacred Books of the East are full of rubbish, and that the same stream which carries down fragments of pure gold carries also sand and mud, and much that is dead and offensive." pp. 112, 113.

"Much, for instance, that is said in the Upanishads about the sacred syllable Om, seems to my mind mere twaddle, at least in its present form." p. 115.

The Professor is most severe on the Brahmanas. Here his "Voice" is "no whisper breathing low." After allowing that they contain "no lack of striking thoughts," he adds:

"These works deserve to be studied as the physician studies the twaddle of idiots and the raving of madmen."

Vedantism is a "satisfying religion" only in the sense of acting as an opiate upon the conscience. (See p. 63).

To the foregoing may be added the opinion of Professor Deussen, of Kiel. Addressing Hindus, he said:

"The Vedánta in its unfalsified form is the strongest support of pure morality, is the greatest consolation in the sufferings of life and death,—Indians keep to it."

Deussen, like Schopenhauer, extols the Vedánta, because he thinks it substantially the same as his own philosophy. There is no material world, all is *máyá*, illusion.

As already mentioned, Deussen, like Ribhu (p. 67) cannot distinguish between "you" and "I", and would tell a beggar who asked alms, "You and I are the same."

It may be noticed that the three favourable opinions quoted are all from Germans. The Rev. Isaac Daniel, B.A. thus explains the German predilection for Hindu philosophy:

"The mind of the typical German is purely *speculative* and not practical, and the ancient Hindu philosopher was exactly of the same caste of mind.

"The great contrast between Germans and the English is this, that while the former are self-centred dreamy, dogmatic, and speculative, the latter are philanthropic, practical, and mindful of truth."

Monier Williams says:

"The more evidently physical and metaphysical speculations are opposed to common sense, the more favour do they find with some Hindu thinkers. Common sense tells an Englishman that he really exists himself and that everything he sees around him really exists also. He cannot abandon these two primary convictions. Not so the Hindu Vedántist."

Max Müller characterizes as "twaddle" and "rubbish" much of what seems "to the Indian mind to contain profound wisdom and to deserve the highest respect."

But the best epithet is that used by one of the most eminent citizens of Calcutta, Dr. Mohendralal Sircar. Addressing a public meeting a few years ago he said :—

"You must have observed a retrograde movement going on in our midst which I fear is calculated to retard the progress of the Hindu race. I mean a return towards superstitions and idolatries which lie as the blackest blot upon this part of the world. The crude words and hazy conceptions of the sages are looked upon as absolute truth. No man is allowed to differ from them however much they may have differed from one another, or however much they may differ from modern science. Indeed, if we are to believe these reactionaries, it is so much the worse for modern science if she will not conform her doctrines to the transcendental nonsense of the sages."—*The Epiphany*, November 5th, 1887.

CONCLUDING REVIEW.

Reasons for the Rejection of Vedantism.

The following may be mentioned:

1. **Its unworthy representations of God.**—Its Supreme Being is unconscious of its own existence. It neither knows nor cares for any one else. It is without love or mercy; it has neither the power to do good or evil—to reward the righteous or punish the wicked. Under the pretence of exalting Brahma, its condition is virtually reduced to that of a stone.

2. **Its blasphemous claims to Divinity.**—Its Great Sentences are, *Tat twam asi; Brahásmi.* The *Brahmavádin* says:

"Man is not the mere creature of a God; he is God himself." "He is himself the Creator."

Such assertions can only be compared to the ravings of a maniac in a lunatic asylum who fancies himself a king.

On the other hand, man is also reduced to the level of the brute. The soul, when it leaves a human being, may next be united to the body of a dog, crow, or insect.

3. **Its denial of the eternal distinction between Right and Wrong.**—The *Brahmavádin* says: "The distinctions of right and wrong are mere appearances which will vanish as soon as the dream-state of life is dispelled." (June 19, 1897). Vedántism thus denies the most sacred convictions of conscience, the highest principle of the human spirit, and cuts at the roots of morality.

4. **Its Physical Errors.**—Vedántism is based on the Upanishads. At page 93 the erroneous accounts given of the human body are noticed. The seven worlds above the earth and below the earth are shown to be imaginary. That some animals are "moisture-engendered" (See page 35), is a fiction.

5. **Its denial of the United Evidence of all our Senses.**—Because a rope in the twilight is mistaken for a snake; therefore all our senses deceive us. The world has no real existence; all is *Máyá*.

6. **Its denial of our Natural Convictions.**—As explained at page 61, we instinctively distinguish between ourselves and the objects around us. Vedántism contradicts this feeling of individuality.

7. **Its flagrant Absurdities.**—The universe contains countless objects, differing widely from each other,—mineral, vegetable, animal. Among the last some are constantly engaged in devouring one another. With what reason can it be alleged that only one Being exists?

According to Deussen, Vedántism teaches that "the soul of each one of us is not a part or an emanation of Brahman, but fully and wholly the eternal indivisible Brahman itself." If this is correct, the number of Brahmans must be countless. Even a musquito is the "eternal indivisible Brahma!" See page 91.

8. **Its denial of the Fatherhood of God and Brotherhood of Man.**—A father is one who gives birth to another. According to Vedántism, we are as eternal as Brahma itself, and therefore have no father. Brothers are children of the same parent. As we have no father, we are therefore not brothers. (See page 95).

9. **Its Selfishness.**—The grand aim is liberation from the miseries of life, to be as useless to others as Brahma itself. On the other hand, the Christian conception of God is, "Thou art good and doest good," and to imitate Him is the great desire of every true Christian. (See page 72).

10. **Its stifling Religion.**—Love, worship, prayer, are three great elements of religion. Vedántism destroys them all. We cannot love a selfish being like Brahma; it is useless to worship or pray to a Being unconscious even of its own existence. (See page 73).

11. **Its Fruits.**—Bishop Caldwell thus asks what has Vedantism done for India, the land of its birth?

"Has it promoted popular education, civilization, and good government? Has it educated the people in generous emotions? Has it abolished caste or even mitigated its evils? Has it obtained for widows the liberty of remarriage? Has it driven away dancing girls from the temples? Has it abolished polygamy? Has it repressed vice and encouraged virtue? Was it this philosophy which abolished female infanticide, the meriah sacrifice, and the burning of widows? Is it this which is covering the country with a network of railways and telegraphs? Is it this which has kindled amongst the Native inhabitants of India the spirit of improvement and enterprise which is now apparent? Need I ask the question? All this time the philosophy of quietism has been sound asleep, or 'with its eyes fixed on the point of its nose,' according to the directions of the Gitá, it has been thinking itself out of its wits. This philosophy has substantially been the creed of the majority of the people for upwards of two thousand years; and if it had emanated from God, the proofs of its divine origin ought long ere this to have been apparent; but it has all this time been too much absorbed in 'contemplating self by means of self' to have had any time or thought left for endeavouring to improve the world. What could be expected of the philosophy of apathy, but that it should leave things to take their course? There is much real work now being done in India in the way of teaching truth, putting down evil, and promoting the public welfare; but that work is being done, not by Vedántists or quietists of any school, but by Christians from Europe, whose highest philosophy is to do good, and by those Natives of India who have been stimulated by the teaching and example of Europeans to choose a similar philosophy."

The Rev. T. E. Slater thus sums up the whole:

"*The Vedánta, the highest conclusion of Indian thought, is based on a mistaken and pessimistic view of life; on a formulated dogma unsupported by any evidence and untaught in the hymns of the Rig-Veda: the whole an elaborate and subtle process of false reasoning.*"[1]

Tennyson thus writes of Pantheism in his *In Memoriam*:

"That each who seems a separate whole
Should move his round and fusing all
The skirts of self again should fall
Remerging in the general soul,—
Is faith as vague as all unsweet;—
Eternal form shall still divide
The eternal soul from all beside."

THE IMPORTANCE OF RELIGION.

The Hindus are fond of speculating about religion, but often they do not realize that it is far more than an abstract theory, that it is a matter which intimately concerns their own well-being both in this life and the eternal unseen world which they must enter at death.

The following remarks of Bishop Caldwell apply to most Hindus, educated or uneducated:

"Practically it matters very little in general what theosophy or philosophy a Hindu professes, what his ideas may be about the most ancient form of his religion, or even what his ideas may be about the religious reforms that the age is said to require. As a matter of fact, and in so far as his actual course in life is concerned, he is content, except in a small number of exceptional cases, to adhere with scrupulous care to the

[1] *Studies in the Upanishads*, p. 47.

traditionary usages of his caste and sect His ideas may have received a tincture from his English education, but ordinarily his actions differ, in no particular of any importance, from those of his progenitors."

Most men are absorbed by pursuit of the present. The insufficiency of this is well illustrated by the following anecdote:

About three hundred years ago, a young man came to a distinguished University in Europe to study law. His long cherished desire was at last gratified. He possessed considerable talents, and commenced his studies with bright hopes.

Soon afterwards, the student called on a good old man, who devoted his life to the benefit of the people among whom he lived. The young man told him that he had come to the University on account of its great fame, and that he intended to spare no pains or labour to get through his studies as quickly as possible.

The good old man listened with great patience and then said:—

"Well, and when you have got through your course of studies, what do you mean to do?"

"Then I shall take my degree," answered the young man.

"And then?" asked his venerable friend.

"And then," continued the youth, "I shall have a number of difficult questions to manage, shall catch people's notice by my eloquence, my zeal, my learning, my acuteness, and gain a great reputation."

"And then?" repeated the good man.

"And then," replied the young student, "why there cannot be a question I shall be promoted to some high office. Besides, I shall make money and grow rich."

"And then?" continued the old man.

"And then," added the young lawyer, "then I shall be comfortably and honourably settled in wealth and dignity."

"And then?" asked his friend.

"And then," said the youth, "and then—and then—than I shall die."

Here the good old man raised his voice: "AND WHAT THEN?" Whereupon the young man made no answer, but cast down his head and went away. The last, "And what then?" had, like lightning, pierced his soul, and he could not get rid of it. The student, instead of devoting his life to the pursuit of the pleasures and honours of this world, sought to promote the glory of God and the good of his country.

Man needs a religion. In youth, in the time of prosperity, the thoughts of God, of death, and a future state, may be distasteful, and the world may be considered sufficient to satisfy the desires. But a change will take place in all. The dark clouds of affliction will overcast the sky; wealth may take to itself wings and fly away; the coveted office may not be gained; health, the absence of which embitters every earthly pleasure, may be broken; loved ones may be removed by death, and, sooner or later, the inexorable summons will reach ourselves.

TWO GREAT RELIGIOUS DOCTRINES.

Space does not permit the doctrines of religion to be described in detail. Two have already been noticed; but on account of their great importance, some additional remarks will be offered.

THE FATHERHOOD OF GOD.

To a child the word *father* represents love, authority, and wisdom. A mother has the same tender affection, but the other qualities are not so clearly shown. Hence, when we seek for a name for God which is most exalted and yet most dear, which expresses love and awe, we call Him our "Father in Heaven."

Two reasons may be mentioned why God is called our Father.

1. **He gave us being.**—As already mentioned, what particularly distinguishes an earthly father is that, under God, he is the author of the child's existence. This can be said of no other person. However much another may love the child and be kind to him, he has no claim to the name of father. Educated Hindus now generally admit the Fatherhood of God, and regard Him as their Creator, but such is not the teaching of Hinduism: it was learned from Christianity. By the word Creator Christians means one who gave being to things which had no being before. In this sense no Hindu sect believes God to have created anything.

According to Hinduism, souls are eternal *svyambhu* essences, without beginning or end, continually in the process of *samsára* or transmigration. We are all little gods as eternal as Brahma himself.

2. **God may be called our Father in heaven because He supplies all our wants.**—A father provides his children with food, clothing, and every thing they need. He does not do so on account of any service they have rendered to him, but from pure love. What has our Father in heaven done for us? He not only gave us life, but He keeps us in life. We are dependent upon Him for every breath we draw; we live upon His earth; it is His sun that shines upon us. Every thing we have is His gift. This is the teaching of Christianity, and Christians therefore praise and thank God for His goodness.

In the above respect Hinduism does not acknowledge the Fatherhood of God. According to it, everything that happens to a person is determined by his *karma*. Every thing that God does to souls He does with reference to their good and evil deeds only, in order that they may receive reward for good deeds, and suffer for evil deeds. The blessings we receive have their source, not in God's benevolence, but in our own good deeds in a previous birth. Why should we be grateful to Him? True religion is thus destroyed.

Early Worship of the Heaven-Father.—It is a very interesting fact that the ancestors of Aryan Hindus and the English once spoke the same language, and worshipped the same God under the same name. Max Müller says:—

"Thousands of years ago, before Greek was Greek, and Sanskrit was Sanskrit, the ancestors of the Aryan races dwelt together in the high lands of Central Asia, speaking one common language.

"The terms for God, for house, for father, mother, son and daughter, for dog and cow, for heart and tears, for axe and tree, identical in all the Indo-European idioms are like the watchwords of soldiers. We challenge the seeming stranger; and whether he answer with the lips of a Greek, a German, or an Indian, we recognise him as one of ourselves. There *was* a time when the ancestors of the Celts, the Germans, the Slavonians, the Greeks and Italians, the Persians and Hindus, were living together within the same fences, separate from the ancestors of the Semitic and Turanian races."

"The Aryans were then no longer dwellers in tents, but builders of permanent houses. As the name for king is the same in Sanskrit, Latin, Teutonic, and Celtic, we know that kingly government was established and recognized by the Aryan at the prehistoric period. They also worshipped an unseen Being, under the self-same name."

"If I were asked what I consider the most important discovery which has been made during the nineteenth century with respect to the ancient history of mankind, I should answer by the following short line:

Sanskrit DYAUSH-PITAR=Greek, ΖΕΥΣΠΑΤΗΡ (ZEUS PATER)=Latin JUPITER=Old Norse TYR.

"Think what this equation implies! It implies not only that our own ancestors and the ancestors of Homer and Cicero (the Greeks and Romans) spoke the same language as the people of India—this is a discovery which, however incredible it sounded at first, has long ceased to cause any surprise—but it implies and proves that they all had once the same faith, and worshipped for a time the same supreme Deity under exactly the same name—name which meant Heaven-Father.

"There is a monotheism which precedes the polytheism of the Veda, and even in the invocation of their innumerable gods, the remembrance of a God, one and infinite, breaks through the mist of an idolatrous phraseology, like the blue sky that is hidden by passing clouds."[1]

"Have we not all one Father? Hath not one God created us?" The Eastern and Western Aryans, after separation for thousands of years, should again unite in the worship of the great Heaven-Father.

---

[1] *Ancient Sanskrit Literature* and *Nineteenth Century*, October 1885.

THE BROTHERHOOD OF MAN.

Brothers are sons of the same father. As already mentioned, according to the Vedánta, we are eternal, self-existent beings. By thus denying the Fatherhood of God, the Brotherhood of Man is also denied.

Dr. John Muir, in his learned work, Sanskrit Texts, (Vol. I), quotes about fifteen contradictory accounts of the origin of man from different or the same Hindu sacred books. This shows that they are untrustworthy. Caste is directly opposed to the Brotherhood of Man. On the other hand Christianity teaches that

> " Children we are all
> Of one Great Father, in whatever clime
> His providence hath cast the seed of life;
> All tongues, all colours."

The differences in colour and features have been produced by the influence of climate, mode of living, and descent.

Although caste promotes a stationary semi-civilisation and has some other advantages, these are far more than counterbalanced by its pernicious effects. To tyrannise over their fellow-beings, the Brahman claimed a divine origin for caste. Dr. K. M. Banerjea well says, "Of all forgeries the most flagitious and profane is that which connects the name of the Almighty with an untruth." Hinduism, to use the words of Principal Caird, "instead of breaking down artificial barriers, waging war with false separations, softening divisions, and undermining class hatred and antipathies, becomes itself the very consecration of them."

Christianity, on the other hand, tends to draw men together.

TWO GREAT DUTIES.

1. **Love to God.**—As already shown, this feeling cannot exist towards Brahma, unconscious of its own existence, neither knowing nor caring for any other being. Christianity, on the other hand, calls it forth in the warmest manner.

Some of the ways in which our love to God will be shown may be mentioned.

1. *A desire to live as in God's presence.*—An affectionate child delights in his father's society. If obliged to leave him, he laments the separation, and wishes to return. So should we feel towards God. It is true that He is always with us, but very often we do not realise His presence. We should live as continually in His sight. We should strive to "walk with God."

2. *A love of Prayer.*—We delight to converse with those we love. Can we conceive of a son, living in his father's house and constantly in his sight, yet never speaking to him, or saying only

a few heartless words at distant intervals? Such conduct would show that he was entirely destitute of filial affection. God is ever near us. We speak to Him in prayer. If we love Him, it will be a pleasure to tell Him all our sorrows, to seek His guidance, and to thank Him for His goodness.

3. *A wish to do God's will.*—If we are attached to a friend, we try to avoid whatever will grieve him, and seek to do what will give him pleasure. Thus it will be with us if we love God. Before doing anything, we shall think how God will regard it, and act accordingly. His laws will be our guide. Obedience is a great test of love. Jesus Christ says, "If ye love me, keep my commandments."

4. *A desire to be like God.*—Children frequently resemble their parents in outward looks; they catch the tone of their voice; they often copy them in their conduct. Even the best earthly parents have their faults, but we are safe in following the example of our heavenly Father. Plato makes "likeness to God" the final aim of man. Jesus Christ says, "Be ye therefore perfect, even as your Father which is in heaven is perfect."

The Hindu idea of "absorption" into the Deity is a great error, but it is our highest duty and privilege to become "partakers of the Divine nature," to be like God, to have our will swallowed up in His. Thus we shall, in some faint measure, share in the Divine happiness.

Such are some of the feelings we should cherish.

2. **Love to Man.**—The "first and great commandment" is to love God with all our heart. The second is to love our neighbours as ourselves. Jesus Christ explained it by saying, "All things whatever ye would that men should do to you, do ye even so to them." This includes the following:

1. *All should be treated with justice.*—The Bible says, "Masters, give unto your servants that which is just and equal." It condemns strongly the rich who oppress the poor.

2. *No insulting language should be addressed to any.*—The Bible says, "Honour all men." Those who have disagreeable duties to perform are entitled to gratitude rather than disdain. Without them cities would be uninhabitable.

The rudeness of some Europeans is a frequent and, in some cases, a just complaint in Indian papers. None regret it more than some of their own countrymen. But the *Times of India* says, "No Englishman treats the Natives of this country with the contempt and insolence which high caste Hindus habitually display towards their low-caste brethren."

3. *We should show our love in every possible way.*—We should sympathise with others in their joys and sorrows. Especially should we seek to comfort them when sick or otherwise afflicted. When they are disheartened, we should try to cheer them; when

they are doubtful what to do, we should give them our advice. We should strive to encourage them in well-doing, while we ought also to warn them against any wrong course of conduct.

It is said of God, "Thou art good, and doest good." God is the happiest Being in existence, and if we had His spirit we should share, in some measure, His happiness. Like him, we should love to do good.

After a life thus spent on earth, Christianity teaches us to look forward to an eternity of conscious happiness in heaven.

Man's Sinfulness.

Nothing perhaps shows more the unfitness of Swami Vivekananda to be a safe religious guide than his denial that man is a sinner.

At Chicago he said :—

"Ye are the children of God, the sharers of immortal bliss, holy and perfect beings. Ye, divinities on earth, sinners! It is a sin to call a man so. It is a standing libel on human nature."

Nearly the whole human race, in all ages, with one voice, acknowledge themselves to be sinners.

The Rig-Veda contains some petitions for the pardon of sin. Varuna is thus addressed:

"Thou, O righteous king, have mercy on me! Like as a rope from a calf, remove from me my sin." II. 28.

In the Atharva-Veda the burden of mental sins is felt:

"Whatever wrong we have committed, sleeping or waking, by ill wish, dislike or slander.

"All these offences, which deserve displeasure, may Agni take from us and keep them distant." VI. 45.

In the Bráhmanas sacrifice is enjoined as the annulment of sin.

Max Müller, referring to the whole continent of Africa, says:

"Wherever we now see kraals and cattle-pens depend upon it there was to be seen once, as there is to be seen even now, the smoke of sacrifice rising up from earth to heaven."

The many millions of Hindus, by bathing in the Ganges and other supposed sacred waters, with one voice, confess that they are sinners.

It is only pride and ignorance that make a man deny that he is a sinner. The holiest men are the first to acknowledge it. Some Brahmans daily make this acknowledgment :—

Pápo'ham pápakarmahám pápátma pápasambhava.

"I am evil; evil in origin; evil-minded; evil in deed."

The Rev. F. W. Kellett, M.A., in a paper entitled, *The Sense of Sin in the Light of History*,[1] shows "that the deeper the sense of sin, the truer the religion."

The two great sins chargeable against every human being are *ungodliness* and *selfishness*.

The verdict pronounced upon Belshazzar, king of Babylon, was: "Thou art weighed in the balances, and art found wanting." The prophet Daniel explained the grounds of this judgment when he said, "The God in whose hand thy breath is, and whose are all thy ways, hast thou not glorified." When conscience awakes, we see nothing in the past but a career of guilt—the grand purpose of our lives neglected, the great God treated with indifference, His holy law trampled under foot. God contrasts the gratitude of the very beasts with the regardlessness of man. "I have nourished and brought up children, and they have rebelled against me. The ox knoweth his owner and the ass his master's crib; but Israel doth not know, my people doth not consider."

Principal Fairburn thus expresses the feelings of every one who reflects seriously on life:

> "Man has noble instincts and impulses that impel him to seek the true, to admire the lovely, to worship the good, to feel after and find the Infinite Perfection in which the true, and right, and beautiful, blend into a divine and personal Unity. Man has deep moral convictions of rights that are his due, of duties that he owes, of an eternal law he is bound to discover and obey. Man has sad and remorseful experiences, the sense of unfulfilled duties, of wasted hours, of sorrows, that have turned the anticipated joys of his life into utter miseries, of mean and unmanly sins against conscience and heart, against man and God, of losses unredeemed by gain, of the lonely anguish that comes in the hour of bereavement and throws across life a shadow that no sunshine can pierce. And out of these mingling instincts and impulses, convictions and experiences, rise man's manifold needs, those cravings after rest, those gropings after a strong hand to hold and trust, those cries for pardon, those unutterable groanings after light shed from a Divine face upon his gloom, in which lie at once the greatness and misery of man."[2]

OUR DUTY AS SINFUL.

If a child has been ungrateful and disobedient, it is his bounden duty to confess his fault, with deep sorrow, and ask forgiveness. This is our duty also to our heavenly Father.

It sometimes happens that an ungrateful wicked son leaves his father's house, and lives among companions like himself, never thinking of his father, and caring nothing about him. Although men have thus acted towards their heavenly Father, His heart still

---

[1] Sold by Mr. A. T. Scott, Tract Depôt, Madras, Price ½ Anna.
[2] *The City of God*, pp. 41, 42.

yearns over them, and He would welcome their return. This is vividly shown in a parable spoken by the Great Teacher, the Lord Jesus Christ:

A certain man had two sons. The younger of them said to his father, "Father, give me the portion of goods that falleth to me." The father then divided all he had between his two sons. A few days after, his younger son went away to a far country, where he soon spent all his property among bad companions. He was now so poor that he went into the fields to feed swine, and he was so hungry, that he would gladly have taken some of the food that the swine did eat.

Afterwards, the younger son thought that, while he was starving, his father's servants had more than they could eat. Then he said, "I will arise and go to my father, and will say to him, Father, I have sinned against heaven and in thy sight, and am no more worthy to be called thy son." As soon as his father saw him coming, he ran, fell on his neck, and kissed him. He told the servants to bring the best robe, and make ready the finest food. Full of joy, he said, "This my son was dead and is alive again: he was lost and is found."

An Atonement needed.—A father may forgive his disobedient children when they are sorry for their conduct and try to be loving in future. It is different, however, with a king or judge. A criminal may be sorry for his conduct, and wish to reform; but he is not let off on that account. If this were done, men would be tempted to break the laws, hoping to be pardoned on their repentance.

The question is, How can God's justice and mercy be reconciled? how can we be forgiven and the honour of God's law maintained?

In all ages the hope has been more or less entertained that God would become incarnate to deliver man from the burden of sin and misery under which the world is groaning. Hinduism has its incarnations. The Kalki Avatára is yet to come, when Vishnu, at the end of the Kali Yug, is to appear seated on a white horse, with drawn sword in his hand blazing like a comet, for the destruction of the wicked, and the restoration of purity.

Christianity also teaches that man is so deeply plunged in sin and his guilt is so great, that a Divine incarnation was necessary for his deliverance. The first promise of this was given by God Himself thousands of years ago. The Son of God, pitying the human race, came down from heaven for our salvation. By His death on the cross He bore the punishment due to our sins; by His obedience to the law of God He wrought out a perfect righteousness, which, like a spotless robe, is given to His followers.

The following illustration has been used: A part of the army of one of the wisest and best of kings conspired against him.

They were seized, disarmed, and condemned to die. The king wished to save their lives, but a free pardon would have tempted others to rebel. The king's only son, who was commander-in-chief of the army, also wished to deliver the condemned men. It was agreed that the prince should suffer punishment in their stead, and when this was done, those who asked pardon in his name would be forgiven.

As the king's son in the parable offered to suffer that the rebel soldiers might be spared, so the eternal Son of God agreed to become man as the Lord Jesus Christ, to suffer and die in our stead. For 33 years He lived on earth, perfectly obeying all God's laws, and at last died on the cross. On the third day He rose from the dead, and afterwards ascended to heaven, where He occupies the highest place of honour. Pardon is now freely offered to all who seek it in His name, accepting Him as their Saviour.

No illustration that can be given fully meets the case ; but the foregoing may give some idea of the way in which God's justice and mercy are reconciled through Christianity.

Objections.—The Christian doctrine of the Atonement has been assailed on various grounds. Some of the objections are diametrically opposed to one another. "By one critic," says Mansel, "the doctrine is rejected because it is more consistent with the infinite mercy of God to pardon sin freely, without any atonement whatsoever. By another, because from the unchangeable nature of God's laws, it is impossible that sin can be pardoned at all." The former would sacrifice God's justice ; the latter His mercy.

Another objection may be noticed. It is maintained that it is unjust that the innocent should suffer for the sins of the guilty. Newman Hall makes the following reply :

"It would indeed be most unrighteous in any earthly ruler, were he to seize an innocent person, and make him suffer the sentence of the law, while the culprit himself was allowed to escape. Supposing, however, the purposes of law were equally accomplished, by an innocent person *voluntarily* submitting to death on behalf of a large multitude of offenders who must otherwise have died, there would be no departure from justice; neither would any alarm be caused to the innocent, by the expectation of being themselves compelled to suffer for the guilty. But if, by such voluntary transference of suffering, those offenders were also reclaimed and made good citizens,—and if moreover he who became their substitute, were restored to life, and as the result of his mediation were raised to higher honour than before, not only justice would be satisfied, but benevolence would rejoice. So with the sacrifice of Christ. He, the righteous, suffered; that we, the unrighteous, might escape. But the act was voluntary. The suffering of Christ was brief, while His triumph is everlasting."

A very erroneous impression prevails among some Hindus. They think that Christianity represents God as angry till propitiated by the Son. On the contrary, the atonement originated in the love of the Father. It was to show that He is a holy God in hating sin, a righteous God in punishing it, and a merciful God at the same time in forgiving it.

Our Duty.—Like the prodigal in the parable, with deep sorrow, we should make the confession, Father, I have sinned, and am no more worthy to be called Thy son." Feeling that we cannot ourselves atone for our sins, nor merit heaven by our best actions which are only like filthy rags, we should take refuge in Jesus Christ, and trust in Him alone for salvation.

While Jesus Christ was on earth, a man, in deep distress, said to Him, "Lord, I believe; help Thou mine unbelief." Though the reader may only be able to

> "Stretch the lame hands of faith and grope,"

let him go to Jesus, saying,

> "Just as I am,—though toss'd about,
> With many a conflict, many a doubt,
> Fightings and fears within, without,
> O Lamb of God, I come!"

Henceforth we should try to live as continually in the presence of our Heavenly Father, speaking to Him in prayer, and trying to fulfil the duties mentioned on pages 122-128.

Sad experience will teach us that we need Divine help to resist temptation and overcome sin. Here the Christian doctrine of the Trinity is felt to be adapted to our needs. Although Christians firmly hold God's unity, yet in some mysterious way there is a Father, Son, and Holy Spirit, who all unite for man's redemption. The peculiar office of the Holy Spirit is to sanctify, to enable us to overcome sin, and to be adorned with all the beauties of holiness. His help is given in answer to prayer. The promise is, "If ye being evil know how to give good gifts unto your children; how much more shall your heavenly Father give the Holy Spirit to them that ask Him?"

Besides prayer for the Holy Spirit, there must be watchfulness against sin, avoidance of temptation, study of the scriptures and other good books, observance of the Lord's day, attendance at public worship, association with good men, etc.

Repentant children are drawn far more closely to God than those who are merely His children by creation. They are His *redeemed* children; Jesus Christ is their Elder Brother. What will He do for them?

They will have a father's *eye* to watch over them. Wherever they are, by day or by night, they can never be out of His sight. They will have the *ear* of a father to listen to their requests. An earthly parent cannot always give his child what he needs, but God has all power. They will have a father's *hand* to guide and protect them. Earthly parents, even though wise, may err; they may be too weak to deliver from danger. Not so with God. They will have a father's *home* to receive them at last. All who love God here will be taken to the "many mansions" prepared for them above, there to dwell for ever.

Thus the beautiful prayer of the Upanishads will be fulfilled:

'FROM THE UNREAL LEAD ME TO THE REAL.
FROM DARKNESS LEAD ME TO LIGHT.
FROM DEATH LEAD ME TO IMMORTALITY.'

In the foregoing remarks, some of the great doctrines of Christianity are only very briefly stated. For fuller information the following are recommended.

Short Papers for Seekers after Truth.—12mo. 112 pp. 1 Anna

Elements of Christian Truth.—12mo. 71 pp. 1½ An. A series. of Lectures by the Rev. Dr. Murray Mitchell.

But the study of the Scriptures themselves is specially urged. A commencement may be made with the *Gospel of Luke*, which was originally written for the benefit of a convert to Christianity, This was followed by its sequel, the *Acts of the Apostles*, written by the same author, which gives an account of the rise of the Christian Church. The two Scripture portions may be obtained in cheap editions at half an anna each at Bible Depôts.

To assist in the study of these two books of Scripture, a little work, *The Beginnings of Christianity*, has been published. Besides an Introduction to the two books, it contains two coloured Maps, and an explanatory Vocabulary of words presenting any difficulty. Price 1½ An. Post-free, 2 As.

The *New Testament* may form the next study. English editions may be obtained at prices varying from 1 to 4 As. An introduction to its study, called *The Founder of Christianity*, intended specially for Indian students, is sold at 4 As. post-free. The vernacular edition of the Scriptures would be helpful to many in understanding their meaning. The complete Bible may afterwards be studied, and even during the whole course portions of it may be read, especially the Psalms.

Evidences of Christianity.—There is an excellent manual on the subject by the Rev. Dr. Murray Mitchell, *Letters to Indian Youth on the Evidences of Christianity.*—12mo. 280 pp. price 6 As. post-free.

Numerous other works are mentioned in the appended Catalogue of Publications.

PUBLICATIONS FOR INDIAN READERS.

Papers on Indian Reform.

This is a Series of Papers treating of the great questions connected with Indian progress—material and moral.

SOCIAL REFORM.

ON DECISION OF CHARACTER AND MORAL COURAGE. 8vo. 56 pp. 1½ As. Post-free, 2 As.

A reprint of Foster's Celebrated Essay, with some remarks on its application to India.

SANITARY REFORM IN INDIA. 55 pp. 2 As. Post-free, 2½ As.

How lakhs of Lives may be saved every year, and crores of cases of Sickness prevented; Precautions against Fever, Cholera, Diabetes, &c.

IS INDIA BECOMING POORER OR RICHER? WITH REMEDIES FOR THE EXISTING POVERTY. 8vo. 82 pp. 2½ As. Post-free, 3 As.

The prevailing idea with regard to the increasing poverty of India shown to be incorrect, and the true means of promoting its wealth explained.

DEBT AND THE RIGHT USE OF MONEY. 8vo. 32 pp. 1 Anna.

Prevalence of Debt in India; its Causes; Evils; how to get out of it; with Franklin's Way to Wealth, &c.

PURITY REFORM. 8vo. 32 pp. 1 Anna.

TEMPERANCE REFORM IN INDIA. 8vo. 40 pp. 1½ As.

CASTE. 8vo. 66 pp. 2 As. Post-free, 2½ As.

Supposed and real origin of Caste; Laws of Caste according to Manu; its Effects; Duty with regard to it.

THE WOMEN OF INDIA AND WHAT CAN BE DONE FOR THEM. 8vo. 155 pp. 4 As. Post-free, 5½ As.

Women in Hindu literature; Female Education; Marriage Customs; Widow Marriage; means to be adopted to raise the position of Women.

THE ABOVE COMPLETE IN ONE VOLUME, 1 Rupee. Postage, 2½ As.

PRIZE ESSAY ON THE PROMOTION OF INDIAN DOMESTIC REFORM. 8vo. 144 pp. 4 As. Post-free, 5 As.

THE SUPPRESSION OF THUGGEE AND DACOITY. 8vo. 56 pp. 2 As.

THE SUPPRESSION OF HUMAN SACRIFICE, SUTTEE, AND FEMALE INFANTICIDE. 8vo. 80 pp. 2½ As.

INDIA BEFORE THE ENGLISH. 8vo. 48 pp. 2 As.

A lecture by R. Sewel Esq. T. C. S. (Retired) showing the condition of the country in ancient times.

RELIGIOUS REFORM.

HISTORY OF THE HINDU TRIAD. (Brahma, Vishnu, and Siva.) 8vo. 64 pp. 2 As. Post-free, 2½ As.

An account is first given of the earliest gods of the Hindus; the changes which afterwards took place are described, with the development of the Triad as given in the Hindu sacred books.

POPULAR HINDUISM. 8vo. 96 pp. 2½ As. Post-free, 3½ As.

Review of the Hinduism, of the Epic Poems and Puranas, &c.; Rites and Observances; Effects of Hinduism, and Suggested Reforms.

PHILOSOPHIC HINDUISM. 8vo. 72 pp. 2½ As. Post-free, 3 As.

The Upanishads; the Six Schools of Hindu Philosophy; the Minor Schools; Doctrines of Philosophic Hinduism; the Bhagavad Gita; Causes of the Failure of Hindu Philosophy.

THE BRAHMA SAMAJ, AND OTHER MODERN ECLECTIC RELIGIOUS SYSTEMS. 108 pp. 3 As. Post-free, 4 As.

Modern Hindu Theism; Ram Mohun Roy; Debendranath Tagore; Keshub Chunder Sen; the Sadharan Brahmo Samaj; Madras Brahmoism; Prarthana Samajes.

INDIA HINDU, AND INDIA CHRISTIAN; OR, WHAT HINDUISM HAS DONE FOR INDIA, AND WHAT CHRISTIANITY WOULD DO FOR IT. 8vo. 72 pp. 2½ As. Post-free, 3 As.

KRISHNA AS DESCRIBED IN THE PURANAS AND BHAGAVAD GITA. 8vo. 72 pp. 2½ As. Post-free, 3 As.

ACCOUNT OF THE TEMPLE OF JAGANNATH AT PURI. 8vo. 48 pp. 1½ As.

CHRISTIANITY EXPLAINED TO A HINDU; OR, THE DOCTRINES OF CHRISTIANITY AND HINDUISM COMPARED. 60 pp. 2 As.

Doctrines about God, Creation, the Soul, Karma, Transmigration, Sin, Incarnations, Salvation, Prospects at death, and Comparative Effects.

SWAMI VIVEKANANDA ON HINDUISM. 8vo. 96 pp. 3 As. Post-free, 4 As.

The Swami's Chicago Address is quoted in full and examined; important facts are brought out which he omitted to state.

SWAMI VIVEKANANDA AND HIS GURU. 8vo. 125 pp. 3 As. Post-free, 4 As.

A history of the Swami and his Guru is given; the Swami's boasted success in the West is shown to be untrue by the letters of 45 prominent Americans; the Vedánta philosophy examined; portraits are given of Schopenhauer and Max Müller, with an estimate of the importance to be attached to their approval of Vedantism.

THE HISTORY OF CHRISTIANITY IN INDIA; WITH ITS PROSPECTS. 8vo. 150 pp. 5 As. Post-free, 6 As.

BARROWS LECTURES. 8vo. 188 pp. 6 As.

Seven Lectures, by the Rev. Dr. J. H. Barrows, on CHRISTIANITY, THE WORLD-WIDE RELIGION.

Descriptions of Countries and Peoples.

PICTORIAL TOUR ROUND INDIA. Imperial 8vo. 116 pp. 6 As. Post-free, 7½ As.

An imaginary tour round India, with visits to Nepal and Cashmere, describing the principal cities and other objects of interest. With 97 woodcuts illustrative of the Himalayas, Calcutta, Benares, Agra, Delhi, Bombay, Madras, &c.

THE INDIAN EMPIRE. 8vo. 215 pp. 6 As; limp cloth, 8 As. Postage, 1 Anna.

A Hand-book of Information for Indian citizens. India, Past and Present, with the work yet to be done, both by Government and people, to render the country prosperous and happy.

THE PRINCIPAL NATIONS OF INDIA. 8vo. 160 pp. 4 As. Post-free, 5 As.

An account of 42 Nations and Tribes of India, with specimens of some of their languages, and 55 illustrations

THE NATIVE STATES OF INDIA AND THEIR PRINCES; WITH NOTICES OF SOME IMPORTANT ZEMINDARIS. 4to. 100 pp. 5 As. Post-free, 6 As.

157 States are described, and 32 portraits are given. The little book will help to enable Indians to understand the vast extent of their country, and what is being done for its improvement.

KASI, OR BENARES, the Holy City of the Hindus. Imperial 8vo. 44 pp. 3 As. Post-free, 4 As.

An account of the city; its Sanskrit schools, ghats, temples, and pilgrimages; with 23 illustrations.

THE BEAUTIFUL GARDEN OF INDIA. 8vo. 86 pp. 2½ As. Post-free, 3 As.

A dream and its Interpretation by a Friend of India. A description of India, Past and Present.

THE GREAT TEMPLES OF INDIA, CEYLON, AND BURMA. Imperial 8vo. 104 pp. with 60 illustrations. 6 As. Post-free, 7½ As.

There are pictures and descriptions of some of the most celebrated Hindu, Sikh, Jain and Buddhist temples; as Puri, Budh-Gaya, Benares, Hurdwar, Gangotri, Ellora, Elephanta, Amritsar, Gwalior, Tanjore, Srirangam, Kandy, Prome and Mandalay.

BURMA AND THE BURMESE. 4to. 54 pp. 2½ As. Post-free, 3 As.

A description of the manners and customs of the Burmese; an account of their government, religion, and history, with illustrative woodcuts, and portraits of King Theebaw and his Queen.

LANKA AND ITS PEOPLE; or, A DESCRIPTION OF CEYLON. 4to. 72 pp. 3 As. Post-free, 3½ As.

The account of Lanka given in the Ramayana is first mentioned. Its history, and present condition are then described, with numerous illustrative woodcuts.

TIBET: THE HIGHEST COUNTRY IN THE WORLD. 4to. 62 pp. 2½ As.

An account of the country, its productions, the curious customs of the people, their religion, and supposed living incarnations; with numerous illustrations.

PICTURES OF CHINA AND ITS PEOPLE. 4to. 56 pp. 2½ As. Post-free, 3 As.

Extent, History, Manners and Customs of the People; Schools, Examinations, Industries; Travelling; Language and Literature; Government; Religions; India and China compared; with 64 Illustrations.

JAPAN: THE LAND OF THE RISING SUN. 4to. 68 pp. 2½ As. Post-free, 3 As.

With 49 illustrations. An interesting description of this beautiful country, and an account of the remarkable changes which have taken place in it.

PICTORIAL TOUR ROUND BIBLE LANDS. Imperial 8vo. 100 pp. 6 As. Post-free, 7½ As.

The principal countries mentioned in the Bible and in ancient history are described; as Palestine, Syria, Babylon, Asia Minor, Greece and Italy; with 104 Illustrations.

ARABIA, AND ITS PROPHET. 4to. 64 pp. 2½ As. Post-free, 3 As.

An account of the Arabs; with descriptions of Jeddah, Mecca, Medina; the History of Muhammad and the early Caliphs; the Koran, Muslim Doctrines, Sects, Prayers, Pilgrimage, &c.; with numerous illustrations.

PICTURES OF RUSSIA AND ITS PEOPLES. Imperial 8vo. 83 pp. 5 As. Post-free, 6 As.

A description both of European and Asiatic Russia, including an account of the different races by which they are peopled, their manners and customs, the Government, &c.; with 89 Illustrations and maps.

EGYPT: THE LAND OF THE PYRAMIDS. Imperial 8vo. 80 pp. 5 As. Post-free, 6 As.

A description of this interesting country, one of the oldest seats of civilization in the world; its ancient religion, its famous temples and other buildings; the manners and customs of the people, etc.; with numerous illustrations.

THE LAND OF SNOWS: with an account of Missions to Greenland. 4to. 56 pp. 2½ As. Post-free, 3 As.

A description of Greenland, so different from India; giving an account of its people; and the efforts to elevate them; with numerous illustrations.

THE OVERLAND JOURNEY TO ENGLAND. 4to. 72 pp. 3 As.

A description of the principal places passed, with some account of the expense, and directions on arrival in England: copiously illustrated.

PICTORIAL TOUR ROUND ENGLAND, SCOTLAND, AND IRELAND. Imperial 8vo. 114 pp. 6 As. Post-free, 7½ As.

Description of the chief places of interest; Public Schools and Universities; Coal Mines and Manufactures; the British Government; Home Life; England an example and warning to India. With 104 woodcuts, and a coloured engraving of the Queen-Empress.

ITALY: ANCIENT AND MODERN. Imperial 8vo. 80 pp. 5 As. Post-free, 6 As.

Remarkable events in the history of the country are described; accounts are given of Rome, Vesuvius, the Buried Cities, and other places of interest; with numerous illustrations.

PICTURES OF WOMEN IN MANY LANDS. Imperial 8vo. 112 pp. 6 As. Post-free, 7½ As.

Descriptions of women, beginning with the most degraded nations of the world, and gradually ascending to the most enlightened; with suggestions, from the review, for Indian women. 172 illustrations.

Biographies.

STATESMEN OF RECENT TIMES. 8vo. 192 pp. 8 As. Post-free, 9½ As.

Accounts are given of the leading Statesmen in the great countries of the world; as Gladstone, Salisbury, Bismarck, and others. Special notice is taken of those interested in India. In all 182 are mentioned, with 122 portraits.

THE GOVERNORS-GENERAL OF INDIA, First Series. By Henry Morris, M. C. S. (retired) 8vo. 145 pp. 4 As. Post-free, 5 As.

Contains sketches of the lives of Warren Hastings, Lord Cornwallis, Sir John Shore, Marquis Wellesley, the Earl of Minto, and the Marquis of Hastings, with portraits. Interesting personal details are given, such as are not usually found in histories.

THE GOVERNORS-GENERAL OF INDIA, Second Series. By the same author, 8vo. 175 pp. 4 As. Post-free, 5 As.

Includes sketches of Lord Amherst, Lord William Bentinck, Lord Auckland, Lord Ellenborough, Lord Hardinge, and the Marquis of Dalhousie.

SKETCHES OF INDIAN CHRISTIANS; WITH AN INTRODUCTION BY S. SATTHIANADHAN, M.A. 8vo. 268 pp. half cloth with gilt title, 10 As. Post-free, 11½ As.

An account of 42 Indian Protestant Christians; Tamil, Telugu, Canarese, Malayalam, Bengali, Hindustani, Panjabi, Afghan, Gujarati, Marathi, Parsi, and Karen; with several portraits.

ANGLO-INDIAN WORTHIES. By Henry Morris, MADRAS C. S. (Retired.) 8vo. 160 pp. 4 As. Post-free, 5 As. Full cloth, gilt title, 8 As.

Lives of Sir Thomas Munro, Sir John Malcolm, Lord Metcalfe, Mountstuart Elphinstone, James Thomason, Sir Henry Lawrence, Sir James Outram, Sir Donald Macleod, and Sir Bartle Frere, with portraits.

EMINENT FRIENDS OF MAN; or LIVES OF DISTINGUISHED PHILANTHROPISTS. 8vo. 158 pp. 4 As. Post-free, 5 As. Full cloth, gilt title, 10 As.

Sketches of Howard, Oberlin, Granville Sharp, Clarkson, Wilberforce, Buxton, Pounds, Davies of Devauden, George Moore, Montefiore, Livesey, the Earl of Shaftesbury, and others; with remarks on what might be done in India.

SOME NOTED INDIANS OF MODERN TIMES. 8vo. 164 pp. 4 As.

Sketches of Indian Religious and Social Reformers, Philanthropists, Scholars, Statesmen, Judges, Journalists, and others; with several portraits.

BABA PADMANJI. An Autobiography. 8vo. 108 pp. 2½ As. Post-free, 3 As.

An interesting account by himself of this popular Marathi author, describing his conversion from Hinduism to Christianity.

PICTURE STORIES OF NOBLE WOMEN. 4to. 50 pp. 2½ As. Post-free, 3 As.

Accounts of Cornelia, Agrippina, Padmani of Chittore, Lady Jane Grey, Ahaliya Bai, Mrs. Fry, Princess Alice, Miss Carpenter, Maharani Surnomayi, Pandita Ramabai, Miss Nightingale, and Lady Dufferin.

THE QUEEN-EMPRESS OF INDIA AND HER FAMILY. 43 pp. 3 As. Post-free, 3½ As.

Her early life; marriage; widowhood; children; progress in India during her reign; traits of character and lessons from her life. With 27 illustrations, and coloured portrait of the Empress.

SIR HERBERT EDWARDES. By Henry Morris. 8vo. 20 pp. ½ Anna.

He is described as the hero of Multan; the peace-maker among wild Afghan tribes; the true friend of India; the earnest Christian.

CHARLES GRANT: the Christian Director of the East India Company. By Henry Morris. 8vo. 48 pp. 1 Anna.

JOHN CHRYSOSTOM: "THE GOLDEN-MOUTHED." 4to. 52 pp. 2 As.

Papers for Thoughtful Hindus.

No. 1. THE RELATION BETWEEN CHRISTIANITY AND HINDUISM. 8vo. 32 pp. By the Rev. DR. KRISHNA MOHUN BANERJEA, late Sanskrit Examiner to the Calcutta University. ½ Anna.

The remarkable resemblances, in some respects, between ancient Hinduism and Christianity are pointed out.

No. 2. THE SUPPOSED AND REAL DOCTRINES OF HINDUISM, AS HELD BY EDUCATED HINDUS. 8vo. 32 pp. By the Rev. Nehemiah (Nilakanth) Goreh. ½ Anna.

It is shown that the belief of educated Hindus with regard to God, His Attributes, Creation, &c., are not found in the Vedas; but have been derived from Christianity.

No. 3. MORAL COURAGE. 8vo. 32 pp. ½ Anna.

A lecture by the Bishop of Bombay.

No. 4. THE IMPORTANCE OF RELIGION. 8vo. 48 pp. ¾ Anna.

An appeal to the young, by John Foster, author of Essays on *Decision of Character.*

No. 5. CHRISTIANITY, OR—WHAT? 8vo. 16 pp. ¼ Anna. By the Rev. H. Rice.

Christianity is shown to be the only religion which meets the wants of man.

No. 6. THE SENSE OF SIN IN THE LIGHT OF HISTORY. A Lecture by the Rev. F. W. KELLETT, M.A., Madras Christian College. 8vo. 20 pp. ½ Anna.

It is shown that the deeper the sense of sin, the more nature the religious life.

No. 7. BISHOP CALDWELL ON KRISHNA AND THE BHAGAVAD GITA. 8vo. 32 pp. ¾ Anna.

A reprint of Remarks on the late Hon. Sadagopah Charloo's introduction to a Reprint of a Pamphlet entitled, "*Theosophy of the Hindus;*" with a preface by the Rev. J. L. Wyatt.

No. 8. THE DUTIES OF EDUCATED YOUNG MEN TO THEIR COUNTRY. 8vo. 16 pp. ½ Anna.

An address, by the Rev. H. Ballantine, at a Meeting of the Ahmednagar Debating Society. Translated from the Marathi.

No. 9. CHRIST THE FULFILMENT OF HINDUISM. 8vo. 23 pp. ½ Anna.

A lecture by the Rev. F. W. KELLETT, M.A., Madras Christian College.

No. 10. VEDANTISM. 8vo. 21 pp. ½ Anna.

By the Rev. Lal Behari Day, with numerous Sanskrit quotations.

No. 11. THE DEFECTIVENESS OF BRAHMOISM. 8vo. 24 pp. ½ Anna.

A Lecture by the Rev. Lal Behari Day.

No. 12. PRELIMINARY DIALOGUES ON IMPORTANT QUESTIONS IN INDIA. 8vo. 74 pp. 2 As. Post-free, 2½ As.

By a member of the Oxford Mission, Calcutta. Hindu and Christian Conceptions of God, Theism *versus* Pantheism, Personality, Merit and Demerit, Sin, &c.

No. 13. HELPS TO TRUTH-SEEKERS. 8vo. 32 pp. 1 Anna.

By the Rev. H. Rice. Current objections to Christianity considered.

No. 14. HINDU PANTHEISM. 8vo. 18 pp. ½ Anna.

From *Anti-theistic Theories*, by Professor Flint, an able writer.

Pice Papers on Indian Reform, ¼ Anna each.

Some are original; others are abridged from the foregoing for popular use.

1. CAUSES OF INDIAN POVERTY.
2. INDIAN MARRIAGE CUSTOMS.
3. SUPPOSED AND REAL CAUSES OF DISEASE.
4. PATRIOTISM: FALSE AND TRUE.
5. MANAGEMENT OF INFANTS.

6. Debt, and How to Get out of it.
7. The Purdah; or the Seclusion of Indian Women.
8. Caste: its Origin and Effects.
9. Astrology.
10. What has the British Government done for India?
11. Who wrote the Vedas?
12. Manava-Dharma Sastra.
13. The Bhagavad Gita.
14. The Science of the Hindu Sastras.
15. Fevers: their Causes, Treatment, and Prevention.
16. Cholera and Bowel Complaints.
17. Animal Worship.
18. Early Marriage; its Evils and Suggested Reforms.
19. Duty to a Wife.
20. The Fruits of Hinduism.
21. Indian Widows, and what should be Done for them.
22. The Advantages of Female Education.
23. Hindu and Christian Worship Compared.
24. Hindu Pilgrimages.
25. Charity: False and True.
26. The Two Watchwords—Custom and Progress.
27. The Value of Pure Water.
28. Charms, Mantras, and other Superstitions.
29. Nautches.
30. Importance of Cleanliness.
31. How to have Healthy Children.
32. How to bring up Children.
33. How to take care of the Sick.
34. Eclipses.
35. Family Prayer.
36. Giving Abuse.
37. Shraddhas.
38. Karma or Fate.
39. The Fatherhood of God.
40. The Brotherhood of Man.
41. Hindu and Christian Ideals on Piety.
42. Prayaschitta.

Complete in a volume, half bound, gilt title, 1 Re. Postage, 2 As.

43. An Appeal to Young India.

Progress.

This is a monthly illustrated Periodical for the educated classes in India and Ceylon. The subscription is only 8 As a year; with postage 14 As. Three copies may be sent for ½ anna postage.

Orders to be addressed to Mr. A. T. Scott, Tract Depôt, Madras.

PRINTED AT THE S. P. C. K. PRESS, VEPERY, MADRAS—1898.